IRQ, DMA, & I/O

RESOLVING AND PREVENTING PC SYSTEM CONFLICTS

Jim Aspinwall

A Subsidiary of
Henry Holt and Co., Inc.

First Edition—1995

ISBN 1-55828-456-7

Printed in the United States of America.
10 9 8 7 6 5 4 3 2 1

MIS:Press books are available at special discounts for bulk purchases for sales promotions, premiums, fund-raising, or educational use. Special editions or book excerpts can also be created to specification.

For details contact: Special Sales Director
MIS:Press
a subsidiary of Henry Holt and Company, Inc.
115 West 18th Street
New York, New York 10011

Trademarks
Throughout this book, trademarked names are used. Rather than put a trademark symbol after every occurrence of a trademarked name, we used the names in an editorial fashion only, and to the benefit of the trademark owner, with no intention of infringement of the trademark. Where such designations appear in this book, they have been printed with initial caps.

Associate Publisher: Paul Farrell
Managing Editor: Cary Sullivan
Editor: Judy Brief
Copy Edit Manager: Shari Chappell
Development/Copy Editor: Gloria Sturzenacker
Production Editor: Joe McPartland

DEDICATION

There are dozens of people to thank for their assistance along the way since I've become exposed to technology, begun to absorb it, and found ways to share it:

- ❖ my parents, Bill and Joan, for everything
- ❖ many close friends and supporters in and out of the computer trade
- ❖ my friends in amateur radio, past, present, and future, for pioneering and bringing technology to the masses before computers became popular
- ❖ my electronics instructor, Bernie, for his dedication to his craft and his students
- ❖ my employers and co-workers at Curtin Call, Hycel, Finnigan, and others for the opportunities to work on so many different things
- ❖ my first PC mentors and fellow authors, Rory Burke and Mike Todd, for their help, insight, and contributions to PCs and their users
- ❖ dozens of on-line friends and acquaintances, from Fran and Art Staniec to Cholo, David, Darrell, John, Bruce, Graham, Charlie, *et al.,* for making this hobby *fun*

❖ Gordon, Elliott, Alan, Rick, Barry, Evan, Brad, Skip, and everyone at DiagSoft for their patience, skills, experience, and exposure to the latest and greatest PC hardware and software technology available

❖ Brenda for the early start in getting published

❖ Judy, Paul, Gloria, and everyone at MIS:Press for helping take our words and making them into something useful and presentable

❖ Kristi, Chris, and Geoff of VNET, and Ron and his students at Branciforte Junior High School (Santa Cruz, California) for the inspiration to convey knowledge of and access to computers to an inspiring generation of new computer users so they can carry on and exceed us

❖ the dozens of people I've come to know in the computer industry, from system board makers to disk drive engineers—constantly challenged and constantly exceeding all expectations in quality and performance

❖ all of my customers and the millions of PC users who need and want more knowledge and information to get through their lives and workdays

My first computer experience was wiring prototypes of Intel 8088 systems for telephony and communications applications from 1973 to 1976. From there I learned to use and fix Alpha-16s, programmed with switches and paper tape. I moved on to LSI-2s, and then on to Data General Nova minicomputers, all hooked up to some amazing scientific research systems. My first computer was an Apple IIc. It did its job and got me away from the typewriter, but I knew there had to be more. After I spent six months of reading everything I could find about PCs and consulting with Rory Burke, my first XT clone appeared, its cursor winking ominously and uselessly until Rory breathed Shareware and "fire" into it (and me) one weekend in 1986.

From that weekend, there seemed to be no stopping the encounters with the on-line world with coaching from Mike Todd, new applications, database programming, and trying to figure out a way to help others enjoy the same experiences. Not until 1991 and my first Pascal course had I ever written a program, and with only two courses of Pascal and one of C, I don't think I'll be making a career of computer programming.

Thanks to an enlightened acquisitions editor at M&T Books, Rory, Mike, and I made it into print, first in 1989 with *The PC User's Survival Guide,* and again in 1991 and 1994 with *Troubleshooting Your PC.* We got the word out and it seemed to help. Challenged by the ever-present need people have to understand and optimize their PC configurations, this latest project came about as much by coincidence as foresight and imagination. This is all a labor of love and appreciation of both technology and the written word, and making good use of them both. After all, sharing our curiosities and our knowledge is the whole point.

My most sincere thanks and appreciation to everyone!

Jim Aspinwall

wb9gvf@netcom.com

CONTENTS

CHAPTER 2

CHAPTER 3

Chapter 4

WONKING, WARPING, AND WINDOWS:
Getting Ready for Those BIG Upgrades 97

CHAPTER 5

Chapter 6

APPENDIX E

APPENDIX F

PREFACE

Reflections and Perceptions about the Quest to Conquer Information for Fun and Profit

Throughout the course of learning about PCs, what they are, what they can do, and how we can make them do it, a considerable amount of before-and-after studying and any number of experiences come to mind.

After reading "all" of the magazines, novice and "techie" computer books, BIOS and DOS guides, and bookshelves bulging with equipment manuals; after seeing millions of new systems ship to their new users; after perusing reports about the thousands of technical support phone calls and e-mails that are exchanged to make all of these systems work, something begins to sink in. I've come upon a number of conclusions or "givens" as I witness and participate in our progress through the initiations that lead to our PC successes:

❖ We've been dealing with the same kinds of problems since IBM first invented the PC.

❖ We *all* have the same or similar problems with PCs.

❖ These problems are solved again and again, thousands of times a day.

❖ We all become experts to some extent, and the experts who are didn't know either, at first.

❖ We will continue to deal with the same kinds of problems for some time—as long as any piece of PC equipment built or software written, at least before the year 2000, is still in use.

❖ Significant changes are yet to come before we can take PCs for granted as we do toasters and VCRs.

Many of the start-up and learning experiences we encounter with PCs seem incredibly significant at the time of enlightenment. Thousands of us know the feeling. A big light suddenly comes on and a loud bell sounds off inside our heads. (Ominous electrical humming sound in the background, ear-splitting *ring*.) "Aha! So *that's* what's going on in there..."

Those seemingly incredible experiences come after hours or days of struggling with some subtle problem, some hidden value or a piece of unresolved logic. Most of the time, it's the heel of one hand or the other making somewhat forceful contact with the center of one's own forehead (causing that ear-splitting ringing and bright light), and the humming sound is a self-effacing "*Duh!*" as it becomes obvious that all we had to do was refer back to the list of resources and rules IBM provided for the PC, check the manuals for our hardware, and play with all the configuration switches and jumpers in some manner as if we knew what we were doing.

Setting up and fixing PCs can be as much dumb luck as it can be a carefully planned, knowledgeable, and quickly satisfying effort. Apparently the thing that makes some people appear to be experts is that they take the challenge seriously enough and aren't afraid to jump in to figure things out—which is usually all that's required. It really does make intuitive sense, to someone, sometime, and if it doesn't, there are rules to start with and to work with along the way.

Sometimes you have no choice but to do it yourself. Sometimes you simply don't want to have to depend on someone else. At other times you get determined to make the upgrade work because the brightly colored, bold-print claim on the box said it was "easy-to-install," and you don't want to go back to the crowded computer store to return the darned thing. Then there's the boss, or your kids, who had so hoped you'd be the hero and get that presentation ready on time or let them play with the dinosaurs before bedtime (and it's already 9:30 on a school night...).

Many of us have been under that kind of pressure, whether it is self-imposed or external. Many of us have made dozens of phone calls and sent volumes of e-mail to our PC-expert friends, emptied many a drink glass and coffee pot, rolled out the sofabed for our guru-guests, or gone home from the office when others were arriving to start their day, just to make a PC work right. When it's all over with, this TV-sized contraption will actually be something that someone can enjoy using. We've been through experiences like this before.

❖ In the 1960s, it was crawling all over the roof to hang that "super color-blaster" TV antenna so we could watch "the big game."

❖ In the '70s, it was a string collector's nightmare of cables, along with plugs, needles, brushes, turntable pads, and 12-inch bass-reflex woofers for the sake of our collection of pop-rock albums.

❖ In the '80s, we pulled out miles of videotape and repeatedly, mistakenly, recorded the shopping channel while trying to figure out how to record our favorite old monster movies at 3 a.m. with our new VCRs.

❖ In the '90s, it's feeding endless piles of diskettes into a narrow slot, and digging invisible black configuration jumper blocks out of the crevices inside our PCs, just to dial up something resembling a chaotic spider web of data to see computer-generated pictures of the White House and the president holding a saxophone on the Internet.

There should be no mystery about the great lengths we go to, feeding that irresistible urge to enjoy new technology. We've repeated these rituals of frustration for years. We probably paid less and expected less back then, but then there was less to get out of it, too.

The PC is just another "thing." It is not to be trivialized, nor are your experiences or frustrations, but you are not and have not been alone in the process. There is always a new term to learn, a new gadget to become familiar with, some assumptions to resolve, and a few dozen combinations of one configuration or another you can get stuck in without a little help from your friends who have been there and done that before. Unless you really want to do something out of the ordinary, there is a solution to almost any problem. It's your decision whether it's worth the cost in time or money to pursue it, or to have someone else do it for you. "I don't know" is a perfectly valid answer—at least it takes you to the next stage: finding someone who does.

Relatively speaking, what we're going through with PCs is no more, no less than any other popular pursuit with gadgets that we've entered into in the past 30 years. If you've finally mastered the difference between *Line In* and *Line Out* at the back of your stereo to avoid that horrendous feedback squeal, and successfully archived those 43 hours of monster flicks on neatly organized racks of videotape during your normal sleeping hours, then what you're encountering now with your PC will be yet another thing to look back on, with pride and humor, during endless hours of eventual productivity and enjoyment. I can't wait until the next decade and the new gadgets it will bring to our lives.

Unfortunately, most of us can't wait until the next decade for the PC to be something we can take for granted. We have to or want to deal with it now. Thus we enter the "Twilight Zone" of PC conflicts and configurations and look forward to a brighter and clearer picture of success with our PCs as the stereo blasts away with classic hits of the '70s and the VCR whirs along recording the last episodes of *Star Trek*. This stuff really does work—eventually!

INTRODUCTION

Welcome to the not-quite-pocket-sized guide to creating and maintaining a clean, high-performance PC *configuration*, or tuning. The thrust of this book is the prevention, or if necesssary, the resolution of what are called *resource conflicts* within your PC system. You may already know what these italicized terms mean (and there is a Glossary at the back), but you may not, or you may need a refresher. In this Introduction we'll provide one, as well as explaining several good reasons to use this book, and how we will go about providing you with clear explanations and directions.

Computer terms can be confusing, so let's be sure what we are speaking of. An IBM-compatible PC *system* is a collection of hardware components, and any software needed to run them efficiently. The hardware in PC systems consists of a set of interconnected components, such as disk drives, a video adapter and monitor, specialized circuit boards, a modem, a printer, computer chips, cables, etc. All these components need rules to make them work together, and the rules are provided by your system's specialized software programs, those stored in either computer chips or on your hard disk. Your *system BIOS* (Basic Input Output System) and your *operating system software* (typically DOS or Windows) together attempt to manage this collection of components. The programs you actually want to use in work or play (word processors, databases, games, and so forth) are called *applications software programs,* and these programs take for granted that your PC has managed its components and resources are managed efficiently, and according to established industry standards each application's own needs. This sounds good so far; but unless all of the components and software are setup properly, and the people installing and configuring them are aware of the rules, conflicts can arise.

An analogy may be helpful here. You probably have a stereo system which also consists of several components—an AM/FM radio, a CD player, a cassette tape unit, an amplifier, a control panel, and speakers. Even if they are all built together in one unit (because of an agreed-on standards in the audio industry) you can expect that all these will work well together if they are connected together and work properly, and that you can play any given CD or tape on any similar system.

Within the PC industry, there is standardization also. This standardization allows for a wonderful, but often bewildering flexibility in components and capacities; but, on the other hand, this flexibility also permits the hardware components in your PC to "bump into" each other when doing their jobs. Furthermore, the software programs that control how your system works also allow great variety in your components and how they work. This software can also cause "arguments" when everything is not properly set up. The bare fact is that the components which make up your PC system have great power and flexibility, but great potential for trouble as well, and the result is that you must investigate and manage all these components from the instant you begin to interact withthe system.

This management job has specialized assets available to it, which we will call its *system resources.* These resources include

IRQs, DMAs, and *I/O addresses*(you may have noticed them in the title of this book), plus many integrated chips and software programs. Don't worry about what these strange terms mean right now; we'll explain them soon. Using these resources, your PC can do a reasonable job of managing itself, but the time will come, if it hasn't already, when you want to change something in it, or a software program (often that whizz-bang new game or multimedia program) changes it for you; some obsure setting will change (or need to), your PC will appear to become confused and uncooperative, and you will likely also become confused (not to mention frustrated).

At this frustrating point you will have to begin to *manage* the *configuration* or setup of your PC system. And at this point we trust this book will be of great help. Of course, prevention is better than cure, so reading the book *now* and taking a few steps will either avoid trouble or help you get out of it easily when it arises. Many of us, by insight or necessity, are taking more direct responsibility for providing our incomes and maintaining our health, and we need to do the same for our PC systems (at least in the short term, but more about that later).

Many of these hardware devices and software programs have many switches and settings. Some of these may be actual little switches (called *DIP switches*) or tiny plugs (*jumpers*) which can be put onto or taken off of tiny little posts. Some devices, like printers, have special software programs (called *drivers*) to control them, which affect how (or even if) they work. Other specialized software, your BIOS, DOS, or Windows, can be set up with various setting, rather like tuning a radio. We will use the term *configuration* to mean which of these possible hardware and software settings are being used in a PC, and as you will see in detail later, there are very specific rules about these settings and assignments. When these rules are broken, *resource conflicts* can arise. These conflicts occur when two parts of your PC system try to share something they can't, like a circuit, a part of memory, or a device, such as a printer port. You may think of your PC's components as a bunch of quarrelling children fighting over toys: "That's mine!" says your modem. "I saw it first!" says your mouse.

These *resource conflicts* can cause things to not work well, not work at all, or even freeze up the entire system. Within this book, we will tell you about the practice of *configuration management* and how you can use it to: determine the current status of your system; avoid conflicts that can cause crashes, errors, or lost functionality; optimize your system for its current use; prepare it for the addition of new devices; and determine if you can successfully install and use the latest operating systems and software.

The information we'll provide applies equally to the one- or two-system user in the home or small office and to multisystem environments. With this book, you will learn how to:

❖ Save several hours of frustration over each potential PC problem

❖ Avoid loss of productive time

❖ Avoid costly technical support calls

❖ Enhance the performance of your system

❖ Speed the installation of new hardware (disks, sound and video cards, CD-ROMs)

❖ Prepare your system for IBM's OS/2 or Microsoft's Windows 95

This is a do-it-yourself guide. There are no complex tools, technologies, or skills required to quickly and easily establish, upgrade, and maintain your PC system configuration. All of the resources you need, with the possible exception of a common screwdriver or two, are contained within your system, its manuals, and this book.

In the process, you will get information that you might have hoped you would never need to know. After all, computers and software are supposed to be more powerful than ever before. PCs do, in fact, do more things a lot faster, but faster does not necessarily mean smarter or better unless the system is set up and tuned properly. And proper configuration requires specific information.

If you want to make toast, you need information about resources and processes. You have to know something about the toaster. While you may not want to design the toaster or make the bread or jam, you need to know how to make the toaster heat up and what to do with the bread and jam. And if you disobey the rules for making toast, your toaster may give you an "error message" like a loud buzzing, or even send you a smoke signal! It is similar with your PC. You should be able to confirm that the pieces of your PC are what they say they are (that COM1: is at the proper address and IRQ, for example; we'll explain what those terms mean later) and that they are working properly. After all, you can call anything "toast," but only if you recognize it as what it is supposed to be, can you know that you actually have it! Similarly, configuration management requires you to collect information from your system and from your hardware and software manuals. Without accurate information, the maintenance of your system will be difficult at best. Unfortunately, the information is often not obvious, or it may be missing.

DISK

We've included a valuable piece of software, DiagSoft Inc.'s QAInfo program, which will identify your system's hardware resources and help uncover many unknowns and possible conflicts that could be preventing the most efficient use of your investment. Also included is a do-it-yourself PC tutorial called What's In That Box, from Jeff Napier. This program will help you identify the physical components of your PC and learn what they do.

Again, this book's intention is to help you prevent and, when necessary, resolve conflicts. A *conflict* within your PC system occurs when hardware, and in some cases software, is configured so that it is trying to use the same system resources as another device or program.

Hardware may conflict by being set up to use the same Interrupt ReQuest (IRQ) signal, Direct Memory Access (DMA) channel, or Input/Output (I/O) address as another piece of hardware. Any one of these resources can be the cause of a conflict. The symptom of a hardware conflict is the inability to use one device simultaneously with another. In such cases, either the entire system or just one or both devices may cease to operate. In some cases, but not all, you may receive an error message from your software or from Windows indicating that some device you expect to be functioning properly is unavailable for use.

Software may conflict with other software or the system by trying to use the same area of memory as another piece of software, which may result in the overwriting of one program's data or program space. Software may also contain unknown or unresolved bugs or conflicts with DOS, Windows, or device drivers; such misbehaved software might try to command an illegal or untimely operation at the microprocessor. Software conflicts are often realized by error messages such as Insufficient Memory, Exception 13, or Windows' infamous

`General Protection Fault` dialog box. Exception errors and General Protection Faults are indicated by memory management software or Windows, both of which monitor and attempt to maintain tight control over the computer's operations. If software for some reason tries to circumvent or improperly control these operations, Windows or the memory manager may warn you—or it may simply freeze the system's operation.

While not a conflict per se, but rather a question of configuration, software might be improperly set up to use the wrong device, or the wrong address or IRQ or DMA channel for a device, and your system consequently indicates a failure to locate or control a specific piece of hardware such as a sound board, COM port, or printer. Configuration management will also help prevent this situation.

NOTE

Memory management configuration and conflict issues are best left to the software and other reference materials dedicated to the subject. We will maintain this book's focus on hardware issues, and when we use the words *system* and *device,* it will be to refer to hardware (and only the software/drivers that enable the specific hardware).

To reach the primary goal of avoiding conflicts, we will take a step at a time—one device, file, or piece of software at a time—and work with the reference information you have or collect, and that which is provided here. You can and will become comfortable with and confident in your system, even if you need to address this issue only once so you can get on with using your PC.

We'll be discussing the standards and assumptions that affect the configuration of your PC, since these are the reference points by which all PC items are set up. We'll discuss the PC and its components as they were, are, and may be in the near future. There is a lot of history, tradition, logic, and reason packed into the design and development of the PC and its various pieces. We are still using many items that were designed according to the technology of anywhere from 3 to 14 years ago. These items are the *legacy* of early PC development, and are called "legacy devices" and "legacy systems." But over time, PCs have become a hodgepodge of old and new technologies, and various attempts to modify or even create new standards have often been poorly or only partially implemented (for example, some were intended as *design workarounds* that tried to use memory addresses or BIOS functions that IBM reserved for possible later use).

The introduction of IBM OS/2, Microsoft Windows 95, multimedia devices like sound cards and CD-ROMs, and also the connection to the world of networks, on-line services such as CompuServe and America Online, and the Internet with IBM-compatible personal computers presents us all with more system conflict challenges. Both OS/2 and Windows 95 provide simpler first-time installation of these powerful, complex environments. But they are still weak in helping you in detecting hardware, reporting device conflicts, and most importantly, offering solutions to problems.

A genuinely new and powerful standard for hardware configuration methods that's now being implemented is *Plug-and-Play* (PnP). It exists only on the newest of PC systems and some applications software. PnP is intended to help resolve, if not eliminate, PC configuration problems by providing the automatic detection and configuration of your system's hardware components. Plug-and-Play technology is built into the *BIOS* (Basic Input/Output System software, which controls the booting up of your PC) of many new 80486 and Pentium PC systems to support both legacy and Plug-and-Play hardware devices. PnP automatically reconfigures your system's PnP-compliant hardware as needed. It does so by detecting non-PnP hardware first, then works around the items it cannot change,, fitting PnP-devices into an optimum configuration. Since most of us are not fortunate enough to be able to scrap our existing PCs, peripherals, and software to invest in all-new Plug-and-Play-compatible tools, we have to deal with both old and new hardware issues.

Even with Plug-and-Play, we are still faced with the problems of setting up our existing PC hardware and software "by the numbers" that represent existing resources we are given. These numbers or resources include the addressing of I/O devices, the IRQ, and Direct Memory Access (DMA) assignments common to all add-in devices. A detailed definition of each of these is provided in Chapter 1.

To help you get your work done in the gap in time between legacy items and the arrival of total Plug-and-Play compatibility, there are many books, software tools, and old hands at this PC trade. You will be introduced to the foundation for using them, learn how to find the information you need, select which information is applicable, and make the most of it.

You will encounter a lot of discussion of both the jumpers and switches (the hardware aspects of a typical PC configuration) and the configuration files (the software aspects). These items are the way the configuration rules we are destined to work with are actually put into practice, at least until every PC system, peripheral device, and software application uses Plug-and-Play or better technology.

There are aspects of PC configurations and hardware that you simply may not want to deal with. If you find this to be the case, you will at least be able, from using this book, to recognize that and seek out the right kind of help from a friend, a service shop, or a technical support phone call. If you find this book to be the long-awaited relief to your PC nightmares, so much the better.

All of this information is primarily to your benefit, and secondarily, perhaps, to the benefit of jammed tech support phone lines. There are a few little-known "secrets" tucked away in here, and we hope to leave you wondering why this book and the tools and information within it aren't packaged with every piece of hardware and software you buy. We could also hope for an unsung "thank you" from the developers of those hardware and software packages for giving their tech support folks a much-needed break. Next time you have to make that call, ask them if they've seen this book!

The first chapter introduces you to the topic of configuration management in depth, its basic steps, and where you fit into the process. As you read further, you will be able to learn about old and new configurations and standards, and the tools that are used in the process. You'll be alerted to the unavoidable limitations of the hardware, software, and the tools to manage them. All of the chapters are rich in reference information and experience, covering from the original IBM PC to the latest in high-speed Pentium technology, new data bus features, Plug-and-Play, and energy conservation.

The ultimate goal is to enable you to control your PC and optimize its performance by using the information and management techniques we provide, thus making you happier and more productive.

In three to five years, all new devices may be Plug-and-Play. We can't wait. We must make the tools we currently have perform the jobs we have today.

CHAPTER 1

CONFIGURATION MANAGEMENT: Planning Ahead

Topics covered in this chapter:

❖ Why a PC system configuration should be managed

❖ Backing up configuration-critical files

❖ Taking inventory

    ❖ Physical inventory

    ❖ System information

        ❖ Interrupt request (IRQ) assignments

        ❖ Direct memory access (DMA) channel assignments

        ❖ Input/output (I/O) addresses

        ❖ Diagnostics

    ❖ Recognizing existing conflicts

❖ Tracking changes to configuration files with REMarks

11

❖ Comments in the **CONFIG.SYS** file

❖ Comments in the **AUTOEXEC.BAT** file

❖ Comments in Windows files

❖ Planning ahead for changes

Your PC's *configuration* is the setting of critical parts of the system so that they work well together. Configuration *management* is the process of planning, tracking, and changing these vital hardware and software settings in your system. Simply put, it is keeping track of what components are in your system, and what changes have been made and why, so that other changes can be made and undone, if necessary—all while keeping your system running smoothly.

Establishing your system configuration occurs at the time your PC is designed and built, by a manufacturer or by you, but *managing* the configuration begins with the person who installs the system and sets it up for use. Managing your PC's configuration requires information about every aspect of your system: the installed hardware and its settings, the *system setup* values (also known as the "*CMOS setup*"), disk partitioning and formatting, and the operating system and applications software. With this information you can discover, resolve, and prevent system conflicts.

NOTE

If you have not done so, we highly recommend that you read the Introduction to this book. Doing so will give you an overview and review of PC systems, give you the benefits of managing your configuration, define important terms, explain the general origin and resolution of PC system conflicts, and set out how this book is arranged. If you read it first you will probably be better able to use the rest of the book, since we will get progressively more into the technical nuts and bolts as we go on.

Properly managing your system configuration should be done (though often is not) every time a change is made to the following elements of your system: the BIOS; the DOS *CONFIG.SYS* file (the first system and DOS configuration file the system encounters at startup); the *AUTOEXEC.BAT* file (usually the first DOS configuration file encountered after DOS loads at system startup); any of your other batch files or device parameters; or when a change is made within Microsoft Windows, OS/2, or other operating environments.

If changes are made to your hardware by adding or removing an option card, memory, cache chips, your CPU, or by changing the address setting on a network or other card, you are dealing with the details of your system configuration. Some of these details will concern the I/O address or IRQ or DMA assignments for one or more hardware devices (more about these soon). What you do to keep track of these details sets the level of management you practice with your system—by doing-it-yourself or hiring the work out (just like whether or not you simply change the oil in your car, or perform major tuneups). We encourage you to spend a little time learning and understanding these details—you will be richly rewarded with peace of mind through a sense of accomplishment.

This chapter will explain the needs and goals of configuration management, and introduce the techniques of vital backups, inventories, diagnostics, and recording changes.

Why a PC System Configuration Should Be Managed

Both the beauty and the curse of PC-compatible systems is that they are so flexible and easily modified by the user. This flexibility provides us many opportunities for interesting and unique working situations, and just as many opportunities for things to go wrong. Configuration management is important to anyone using or supporting a PC system.

Most systems sold today are preconfigured at the factory, but many of us still buy components and build our own systems. Even after obtaining a factory-built system, we find ourselves replacing, adding to, or upgrading one or more system components with off-the-shelf items purchased from the local computer store or by mail order. Replacement components sent by system manufacturers usually require some modification of settings as well. Some software and hardware we buy changes our configuration settings when we install it, often without our knowledge or permission. Any of these changes can result in malfunctions or no functions at all. We can lose time, money, and our data (sometimes the most valuable of the three). Thus configuration management is critical to us as individual users, dealing with a variety of hardware, software, and operating systems, as we all are. And it is especially valuable when more than one PC system is involved. Some of the more significant benefits of configuration management are:

❖ Greater reliability

❖ Less wasted time when modifying PC systems and solving problems

❖ Preparing for upgrades to hardware or software

❖ Tracking equipment and software for security, expense, and tax purposes

❖ Software licensing and copyright compliance

Your goal may be as simple as getting all of the components in your system to operate together correctly—you want your system to be safe and stable. After all, whether you are working or relaxing with it, you want your computer to work right. You want to establish and maintain *reliability*. As we mentioned, some software installations alter your configuration files or the settings of your modem, video card, or software-configured devices, and this changes the way things worked before, so you also want to be able to reconstruct your system and get back to work quickly in case something fails or becomes corrupt—you want to recover efficiently. Reliability, efficiency, and maintaining good records for insurance, expense management and taxes are very important issues for any user. If you share your system with other users, or if someone else is responsible for maintaining your system (with or without your presence or immediate awareness), reliability and efficient recovery cannot be overemphasized.

Considering that many users and companies will be upgrading to higher-performance components and operating software, it is important to know if existing PC systems are capable of all the tasks required of them, if software or hardware upgrades are warranted, and if they are even possible. For the user considering using IBM's OS/2 or Microsoft's Windows 95, you will save yourself a lot of time and frustration by making sure you know what components are in your system, how they are set, whether the system is properly configured, and how to correct configuration problems, so that any upgrade work can proceed smoothly and successfully. You can trust installation software just so much, and you should be able to determine if it has misidentified or failed to identify a critical component in your system.

All of these issues apply regardless of whether one system is used or many. But with one or many systems, there are more considerations. Whether in a single office or throughout an entire corporation at one or more locations, it is more efficient to have the systems configured as alike as possible for easier support, and it is necessary to have reliable information about them. Managing the configuration by locking the covers on the box and write-protecting critical files is one approach, but it does not do enough (especially if the system is locked down in an improper configuration!).

For a 10- to 30-system office, where only a few systems may be used and configured differently, keeping track may be fairly simple. Managing the configuration of hundreds of systems, even by more than one or two people, is a significant task that requires planning, good procedures, and discipline. The fewer systems you have that perform different functions, with few or no specialized configurations to suit those functions, the easier it is to maintain them—but you still need to have the data about each of them.

Fortunately, configuration management for any number of systems, from one to hundreds, consists conceptually of just a few basic procedures.

The first steps you must take to manage system configurations must insure the reliability of the hardware, software, and configuration file items within your system. This means system inventories and frequent and regular backups. The original configuration should be recorded and saved for future reference. Then, as you make changes to the system (such as upgrading or adding components), record these changes. With this information you can trace the changes and reestablish the original configuration, if need be. Let's explore these steps in turn.

Backing Up Configuration-Critical Files

Before doing any work on your system, you should make backup copies of all the files necessary to your system configuration. As changes are made, these files may also be changed, and it's possible that one or more configuration changes will fail. Recovering from such failures is much easier if you can go back to a set of configuration files that allowed the system to work properly. These copies may be kept on the system's hard disk, or better, on a marked diskette dedicated specifically to this purpose. If you keep these files on a diskette, you should put the operating system on it (either with a command similar to **FORMAT A: /S** or by putting the diskette in the drive and typing **SYS A:**). Then it will be easier to access DOS if you encounter problems with your hard disk during reconfiguration. Ideally you should maintain complete and current backups of all the files on your system's hard drives on tapes or diskettes, because sooner or later you *will* need them, but at the very least, have copies of the critical configuration files which are vital to get your system up and running properly.

The minimum set of files for which you should keep backups is:

❖ **CONFIG.SYS** (found in the Root directory of your C: drive)

❖ **AUTOEXEC.BAT** (found in the Root directory of your C: drive)

❖ **WIN.INI** (found in your Windows subdirectory)

❖ **SYSTEM.INI** (found in your Windows subdirectory)

❖ **PROGMAN.INI** (found in your Windows subdirectory)

❖ **CONTROL.INI** (found in your Windows subdirectory)

CONFIG.SYS and **AUTOEXEC.BAT** almost always refer to other programs, since their job is in effect to tell your system exactly how to set itself up as it comes to life. Your video card, your printer, your CD-ROM drive—these and other system functions may require their own special programs or drivers. Thus you should also include all of these other files in your backups, so your PC can find them and run them as it boots up, at least to the DOS level (Windows versions before Windows 95 run "on top of" DOS).

You may also wish to keep copies of all of your Windows .INI files (those with the extension of .INI after their filename) and your Windows Program Group files (those with the extension of .GRP after their filename). Windows and its applications use .INI files to store a variety of configuration settings, which define how they function and appear on screen. The .GRP files define each of the major folders on your Windows desktop, and contain application and file references. Without these .INI and .GRP files, you may get Windows running, but you may have to do a lot of reinstallation and tinkering to get everything working right again. Copying back a few files is *much* easier!

If you are running a network you may also wish to keep a copy of your network configuration file (typically **NET.CFG**) with your backup files.

Do you have *current* copies of these files? If not—please make them NOW on labeled diskettes. Include today's date. If you're not sure if any copies you have are current, *make new ones!*

Taking Inventory

The next important step you need to take is to inventory your system. This includes both a physical inventory and a "configuration" or "software" inventory, covering these items:

❖ a list of all your hardware items

❖ a list of all your software and configuration files

❖ all of the manuals for your hardware and software (stored together in a convenient place)

❖ hardware-specific software and data files (on their respective diskettes) gathered together

This inventory allows you to establish a baseline indicating the present condition of your system. In the process, you may discover items that are misconfigured (according to standards or certain rules that apply to PCs).

In multiple-system situations, inventory may also be taken by the system administrator or computer support department where you work. Some of this information can be retrieved automatically during routine system and network maintenance. It is in their best interest as well as yours to maintain system inventories, for all the reasons stated earlier, as well as for network management.

Physical Inventory

A hands-on, physical inventory of your system and system configuration information should be performed when you first buy, unpack, or build your system. Do it now if you haven't already! You should have both a written/printed and a data-file record of all the makes, models, versions, serial numbers, descriptions, and technical support numbers of the components in and around your system. This includes everything from the power supply to the mouse, from the hard drive adapter to sound and multimedia cards. Allow enough paper and leave extra space, and put the written and printed sheets in their own special folder. Keep it safe but within easy reach.

There are a number of things to keep in mind when you open up your system:

❖ Have a flat workspace with plenty of room and light.

❖ You'll need a Phillips and a flat-blade screwdriver, a flashlight, and a container to store screws.

❖ Have some masking tape, blank paper, and pen ready.

❖ Remember that you can damage delicate electronics. Prevent static discharge onto components by wearing an anti-static strap.

❖ Make simple but clear sketches of where things are at each successive stage, *before* you remove anything! This includes any cables at the back of your system as well as in it.

❖ Don't remove cards and cables unless it is necessary; label them with masking tape as you go. Note how connectors and plugs are lined up.

❖ Don't remove any chips! You can use a small piece of tape on most chips as may be needed.

It is a good idea to make 2 copies of everything, and keep a copy at a second location. This copy will be invaluable in the event of fire, theft, etc.

T I P

For your system board and add-in cards, note the numbers printed on any labels that are attached to the tops of chips or the boards. (See Figure 1.1 for a map of the inside of your computer's "box," where chips and boards will be found.) These numbers likely reflect revisions of BIOS (Basic Input/Output System) for the system, for *SCSI (small computer system interface)* host adapters, video adapters, and sound cards (some of these numbers are visible on-screen during system startup, or appear on a label on the boards themselves).

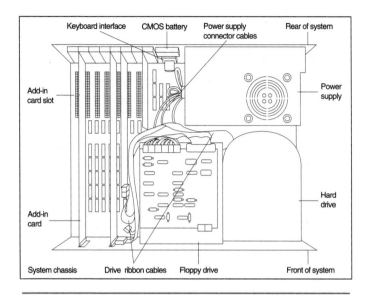

Keyboard interface   CMOS battery   Power supply connector cables   Rear of system

Add-in card slot

Power supply

Add-in card

Hard drive

System chassis   Drive ribbon cables   Floppy drive   Front of system

Figure 1.1 YOUR PARTICULAR SYSTEM MAY DIFFER SLIGHTLY FROM THAT ILLUSTRATED HERE, BUT IF YOU HAVE AN *IBM PC* OR COMPATIBLE MACHINE, IT LOOKS SOMETHING LIKE THIS INSIDE.

T I P

Most boot-up screens can be paused so you can read and copy the otherwise fast-scrolling information. Usually the PAUSE key will suspend the boot-up process, and the SPACE bar will allow the process to resume. See your system manual, or watch the screen closely as the system boots for the keystrokes you need.

WARNING

Most system (BIOS or CMOS) setup routines can be accessed during boot-up. YOU SHOULD AVOID MAKING CHANGES AT THIS LEVEL unless you are familiar with the various parameters. It is possible to *seriously* misconfigure your system beyond your ability to recover! You must take *great care* on how you *exit* a setup screen. Be sure you are making no changes as you leave the setup program unless you intended to make them.

A typical physical inventory list might look like this:

System Make/Model:	Gateway 2000 4DX-25
System Board:	Micronics Gemini Local Bus (Model and Serial #)
System BIOS:	Phoenix/Gateway GLB-05
Power Supply:	250-watt AT-desktop style (Mfr., Model, and S/N)
CPU:	Intel 80486DX-25Mhz
RAM:	4 ea. 4M 32/36-bit 80nSec SIMMs
Hard Drive Adapter:	On-board IDE (wired into the system board)
SCSI Adapter:	Adaptec 1542B
Hard Drive:	Western Digital Caviar 220M IDE (Model and S/N)
CD-ROM:	Toshiba 3301 SCSI (Model and S/N)
Diskette Drives:	Sony 3.5" 1.44M (Model and S/N)
Diskette Controller:	On-board (wired into the system board)
Video Adapter:	Diamond SpeedStar 24x, VESA BIOS 1.1 (S/N)
Video Monitor:	Panasonic PanaSync C1381i (S/N)
Ports:	COM1 (on-board, 2nd port disabled)
	COM2 (clone add-in w/ 16550 UAR/T) (Model and S/N)

	LPT1 (on-board)
Mouse:	Generic trackball, serial interface
Network Card:	Clone NE1000-compatible, BNC connector
Modem:	USRobotics Sportster 28.8 (S/N#1234567890) Fax on COM2 Internal Version #12345 DSP Version #9876
Keyboard:	Northgate OmniKey/Plus (S/N#56a98)

OTHER REFERENCE

Additional modem-specific information may be obtained by using software to "look inside" the modem. A program such as Hank Volpe's Modem Doctor, which is available from many BBSes and on-line services, or nearly any communications software (COM-AND, Qmodem, or even Windows' Terminal) can be of great help identifying your modem, especially if it is an internal model.

You can often get your modem to identify itself by running your communications software running in direct or terminal mode. Consult your modem manual or help file for how to enter terminal mode (this is *not* the same as running terminal-emulation software within Compuserve or another on-line service). If you key in the command **AT13[Enter]** and wait for a response, then type in **AT17[Enter]**, you should see a display similar to the following:

```
at13[Enter]
Sportster 28800/Fax V6.0
OK
at17[Enter]
Configuration Profile...
```

```
Product type          US/Canada External
Options               V32bis,V.FC,V.34
Fax Options           Class 1/Class 2.0
Clock Freq            20.16Mhz
EPROM                 256K
RAM                   32K
Supervisor date       11/30/94
DSP date              11/29/94
Supervisor rev      ˙ 6.0.4
DSP rev               1.0.5
OK
```

The first line after the **AT13** command usually returns the modem's model number. The last four lines shown here, not including the OK, are typical pieces of information that the modem manufacturer may ask you for during a support call. Major manufacturers such as Hayes, USRobotics, Supra, Practical Peripherals, Intel, and AT&T provide these internal facts to help with either manual or automatic identification of modems, which can be very useful during automatic setup of communications and facsimile programs. Clone or no-name "white box" modems may not be as helpful.

In addition to identifying the various devices in your system, you should also record their settings or positions of the jumpers and switches. Making that little diagram showing these settings, or marking them in the manual now could be a lifesaver later if you have to change something to resolve a conflict. It's also a good idea to clearly label each device and all its settings. Using a nonconductive, self-adhesive, removable paper label or piece of tape attached directly to the device is an excellent way to keep a convenient and accurate record.

If you can locate the associated diagrams in your manuals, compare the settings. If they are set to their factory defaults, make a note to that effect.

T I P

System Information

To properly manage a PC configuration, besides basic information on your hardware, you need at least three other specialized types of information about the system board and add-in devices in your PC. These are so vital to configuration management that this book's title is based on them: *IRQ, DMA, & I/O.*

Let's get some basic definitions on the table first.

Interrupt Request (IRQ) Assignments

These are signal lines connected between a variety of devices, both external (through add-in cards) and internal to your *system board* (which contains the *central processing unit [CPU]*, or main computer chip; the *RAM* [Random Access Memory] chips and other chips, like the BIOS; and the connections for built-in and external devices). Using these IRQ signals, devices such as the serial (COM) port, keyboard, sound card, and disk drive signal the computer that the device needs the CPU's attention to move data, perform a job, or handle an error situation.

Direct Memory Access (DMA) Channel Assignments

A DMA channel is a set of two signal lines, one line for DMA request (DRQ) and the other for DMA acknowledgment (DACK), assigned in corresponding pairs (as a single DMA channel assignment) to devices that have the ability to exchange data directly with system memory or RAM without going through the CPU. DMA stands for *Direct Memory Access.* Via a DMA channel, a device signals the CPU that it wishes direct access to another device, usually system memory. The CPU then gets out of the way, and the DMA data transfer is performed under the control of the devices themselves. Its advantage is that it is very fast, much faster than if the CPU and software handled the operation (although it does cause the CPU to stop processing

25

for a short time). Many disk drive and tape drive functions and multimedia cards use DMA for faster data transfer.

Input/Output (I/0) Addresses

We'll talk about these in a minute, but for I/O addresses to make sense, we should explain a bit about memory. A great deal of a PC's actual work involves moving data around the system and performing operations on it—making computations, storing characters, displaying pixels on your monitor screen, and so forth. This data is stored mostly on your disks or CD-ROM until it's needed, and when you save a letter or database file, the data is put into storage in an orderly manner, so that it can be found and used when needed. Besides your disks, your PC has another place it stores data, but unlike the disks, data is only stored there while your system is running. This big pool of memory is called *system memory* because your *system* has use of it, and called *RAM* because it is *Random Access Memory* (i.e., any of its millions of "slots" or locations can be checked as needed). These locations in memory have specific uses or assignments, as it were, so that all the complex transactions that your system needs to run can take place efficiently. Locations in memory are called *addresses*.

Input/Output devices are those which send and receive data in order to do their jobs, like modems, printers, mice, keyboards, video and sound cards, and so forth. *Addresses* are numbers which point to the actual memory locations used for the *data bus* (the 8-, 16-, or 32-bit data lines within the computer) for interconnecting devices or system memory. *Addresses* are used to identify the unique places in your system where data and control information can be exchanged between devices, the CPU, and system memory. Each Input/Output device, such as a serial port or disk drive, is said to occupy a specific I/O *address* or location in memory. Only data or commands intended for that particular device's address should be sent to or expected from its location. If some other device is assigned the wrong address and the "rightful" device checks its slot and finds another there—well, we begin to see what the phrases "resource conflict" and "device contention" mean!

When we talk about resource conflicts, however, we are *not* speaking of conflicts between our Big Three resources *themselves*. IRQ, DMA, and I/O are mutually exclusive in that one is not dependent upon another (except in some specific cases) and thus they don't conflict with each other (IRQ1 doesn't conflict with DMA1, for example). Nevertheless, these three can be closely related, as we will discuss in Chapter 2.

You may also need to know the memory location of a particular device's internal BIOS, known as the BIOS address (which may also be referred to as the "ROM address" or "ROM BIOS address"). This information is usually standardized, though there can be many variables, typically in the BIOS address for the SCSI host adapters used to connect disk, tape, scanner, and CD-ROM devices.

Add-in devices such as video display, disk drive, network, and SCSI host adapters each contains its own BIOS (Basic Input/Output System). The BIOS in this case is a special program that is used to provide compatibility or added features that help make the device work with the rest of your computer system. In many ways this is similar to the system BIOS we mentioned above, the internal program used to start up and initially configure your PC so it can run your operating system.

When your system starts up, it must run the system BIOS, which will in turn cause any add-in device BIOS programs to be run as part of the system boot-up. These programs require their own addresses and portions of memory, in addition to those used for the hardware I/O signals. The addresses for the BIOS built into add-in devices, especially SCSI host and network adapters, require some configuration adjustment because they can conflict with each other. The address for the BIOS on video and non-SCSI disk drive adapters is usually assigned to a specific address and cannot be changed. We will discuss more about these addresses in Chapter 2.

Diagnostics

If you think technology should take care of itself, that you have no need for the technical details of your system, and that diagnostic tools such as the Norton Utilities are for someone else, the time has come to reconsider. Ready or not, you are in the market for some diagnostic or utility software.

To get the IRQ, DMA, and I/O information requires one or more pieces of software for gathering information from your system, possibly a closer physical inspection of the hardware to find labels or markings, and also the manuals for your system and add-in cards as critical references to help you isolate and make note of these settings.

Even Microsoft, one of the world's largest software companies, saw the need for a technical information tool to help with software support. In an attempt to fill this need, Microsoft created MSD, the Microsoft Diagnostics. It will give any user a basic snapshot of generic system hardware by device type (See Figures 1.2 and 1.3).

Figure 1.2 MICROSOFT MSD'S BASIC SYSTEM INFORMATION SCREEN.

```
File  Utilities  Help
                          IRQ Status
 IRQ  Address    Description        Detected      Handled By

   0  0CCD:0382  Timer Click        Yes           TXT2PCX.COM
   1  0CCD:03DE  Keyboard           Yes           TXT2PCX.COM
   2  0133:0028  Second 8259A       Yes           QEMM386
   3  0133:002C  COM2: COM4:        COM2:         QEMM386
   4  0132:0030  COM1: COM3:        COM1:         QEMM386
   5  0132:0034  LPT2:              Yes           QEMM386
   6  0132:0038  Floppy Disk        Yes           QEMM386
   7  0070:05B0  LPT1:              Yes           System Area
   8  0119:01C0  Real-Time Clock    Yes           QEMM386
   9  0119:01C4  Redirected IRQ2    Yes           QEMM386
  10  F494:01CB  (Reserved)                       BIOS
  11  D3C5:410A  (Reserved)                       SCSIMGR$
  12  0118:01D0  (Reserved)                       QEMM386
  13  0118:01D4  Math Coprocessor   Yes           QEMM386
  14  0118:01D8  Fixed Disk         Yes           QEMM386
  15  0118:01DC  (Reserved)                       QEMM386

                          OK

IRQ Status: Displays current usage of hardware interrupts.
```

Figure 1.3 MICROSOFT MSD'S IRQ INFORMATION SCREEN.

OTHER REFERENCE

MSD is available with many Microsoft product packages or for downloading from on-line services such as CompuServe and America Online. Microsoft wants you to have this program to make its own technical support life easier. That a software company found itself needing hardware information to support software packages should tell us something about the tremendous universal need for technical information about our PC systems.

A preconfigured PC system may come with diagnostic software. Well-defined hardware add-in kits, such as multimedia adapters and network adapters, embed system information utilities such as these into their installation programs.

OTHER REFERENCE

If your system did not come with diagnostic or utility software, aftermarket programs such as Symantec/Norton's SYSINFO and Quarterdeck's MANIFEST are available as part of other utility software packages (Norton Utilities and Quarterdeck's QEMM respectively). (See Figures 1.4 and 1.5.) Still others, such as SysID by Steve Grant, can be found in online system libraries as public-domain software or shareware. (See Figures 1.6 and 1.7.) These all provide basic configuration information.

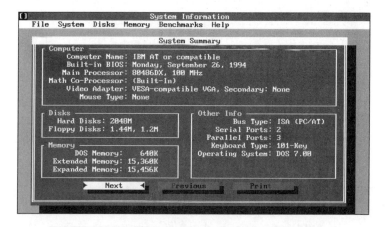

Figure 1.4 NORTON UTILITIES' SYSTEM INFORMATION SCREEN.

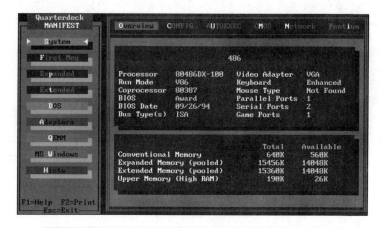

Figure 1.5 QUARTERDECK'S MANIFEST SYSTEM INFORMATION
SCREEN.

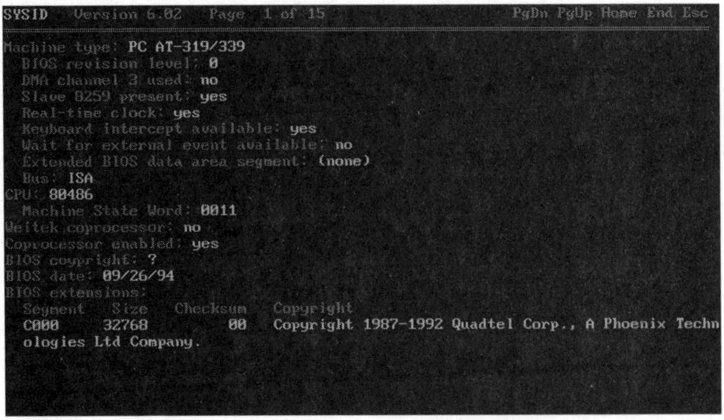

Figure 1.6 *SysID's SYSTEM INFORMATION SCREEN.*

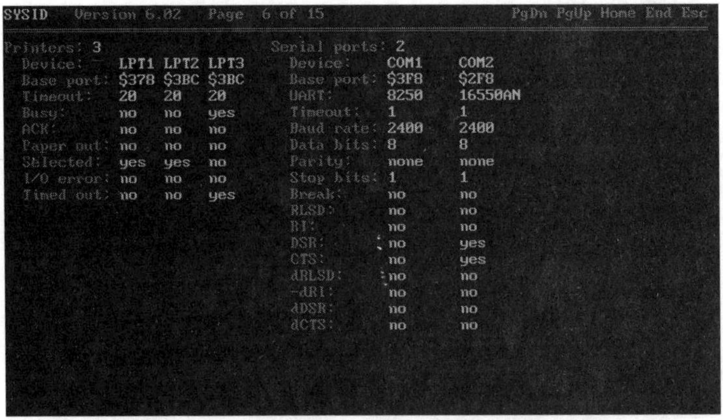

Figure 1.7 *SysID's I/O PORT INFORMATION SCREEN.*

Because of the complexity of systems and the variety of add-in devices available, however, many of the commonly available utilities miss or simply do not provide important details, or they give incorrect information or "guess wrong." You might have to use more than one of these programs to ensure that most or all of the devices in your system are properly detected, and to confirm any possible irregularities.

For a more accurate and complete identification of system hardware and resource usage than many other programs provide, a copy of DiagSoft's QAInfo program is included with this book.

DISK

QAInfo is developed and frequently updated in close cooperation with many PC device and system manufacturers, often at their request, for their own uses. This program, accompanied by the specific details in your add-in device manuals and a physical inspection of the hardware, will give you a complete picture of the existing system, and of changes as you may make to them. (See Figures 1.8 and 1.9.)

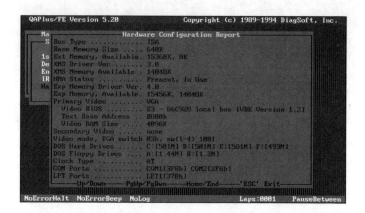

Figure 1.8 DIAGSOFT QAINFO'S HARDWARE CONFIGURATION SCREEN.

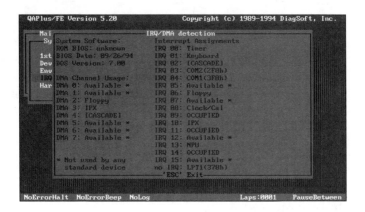

Figure 1.9 *DiagSoft QAInfo's IRQ and DMA*
INFORMATION SCREEN.

Any system information program can only find and report on the devices they are designed, through extensive research, to identify, and then only if these devices are functional. You will get a report of the functioning devices that exist and the resources they use. Diagnostic software cannot report on devices that physically exist but are defective or inactive, nor can it report conclusively on whether a resource is available, unused, or otherwise unoccupied. By a process of comparison you can identify the resources (I/O addresses and IRQ and DMA assignments) that remain available to you, and we'll be helping with that process as we go along.

People who support multiple systems will likely use network-management-specific tools to perform many of these inventory and tracking functions, but may use DiagSoft's QAPlus-family of diagnostic software, which includes the features of QAInfo, or similar products for individual workstation support.

Using at least one of the programs mentioned here, or similar ones, gather and record all of the information you can get about your system. Most programs provide the ability to print the information or store the information in text files on disk. Keep this information with your physical inventory and settings records. We will go into more detail in the following chapter; basically, you will compare the information you collect with the "rules" and information provided in this book. From this comparison, you will have the information you need to assess your present configuration and correct it if necessary. You will also (by the process of recording assignments) identify the resources you have availble for any modifications you want to make to your system.

Cleaning Up Existing Conflicts

If, in the process of gathering the physical and "soft" inventories of your system, you encounter any configuration questions or conflicts, now is the time to correct them. Indeed, the purpose of this book is to help you do just that. Many tables and explanations of proper configuration are contained throughout, and also exist in numerous hardware and software manuals. Some of the adjustments also require you to refer to drawings and tables that may be found only in the vendor's documentation, on-line help, or downloadable support files (available on their electronic Bulletin Board System or in their section on a service such as Compuserve).

There are aftermarket books and support files that contain references to many common PC components, such as system boards, disk drives, disk drive adapters, and video adapters. These may be your only source of reference for some components. There are also many "no-name," generic, or "white box" components that have no manuals and no easy means to obtain them from the original manufacturer. Such clone devices, and those of off-shore origin, are plentiful and have provided us with a steady flow of inexpensive components. But they are not inexpensive when you cannot support them. If you can't find the original documentation, your best bet is to replace the device and make sure you save the new manuals in a safe place. You might also nag your vendor, who may be able to mail or fax you a copy.

Recording Changes to Configuration Files

In addition to backing up your critical configuartion files, it is excellent practice to have a way of recording notes about them and changes to them right in the files themselves, where you'll always be able to find them. Adding REMark or comment lines within the configuration files to highlight and explain the changes is a positive and highly recommended step in configuration management. You will find that many programs which make modifications to your setup files also add their own unique comments for your possible use later. Then again, many do not; if you do, it will be easier to review, decipher or modify later.

Since all of these files are ASCII text files, any basic *text editor* (a program that creates, reads, and saves files in plain ASCII text, without regard for type style or size, justification, etc.) can be used to create, edit, and add comments to them. Under DOS (from version 5.0 on), you can use the DOS **EDIT.COM** program. Under Windows, you can use the **NOTEPAD** program, usually found in the Accessories program group.

Do not attempt to use programs or tools, or to change files or commands, that you are not familiar with—especially without a backup of a working file. You should be familiar with, or refer to, DOS- and Windows-specific documentation for the finer points of text editors, DOS commands, batch files, and command-line structures, which will be illustrated in this section.

Don't be concerned right now about how the specific command lines used as examples in this section would affect your configuration—they're only used to illustrate the process of commenting on changes. Again this warning: make new backup copies of at least the setup and configuration files on your system, if not your entire hard drive system, before making changes.

To make a backup of your **CONFIG.SYS** file, for example, use the DOS **COPY** command to copy your working **CONFIG.SYS** file to a similar filename. Pick a filename that is easy to remember, and one that would not likely be overwritten, deleted, or used for another purpose. Using the original filename and a unique extension such as your initials usually suffices, as shown below. For this example, you must be in the root directory (the highest-level directory) of your boot drive, assuming your boot drive is C:.

If in doubt, at the DOS prompt, key in: **C: [Enter],** then key in: **CD \ [ENTER]** to get to the root directory. Then key in the following: **COPY CONFIG.SYS CONFIG.JA [Enter].** If you are saving to a diskette, insert the letter of your diskette drive, followed by a colon and backslash, in front of the destination filename. If you're saving to drive A, you would type: **COPY CONFIG.SYS A:\CONFIG.JA [ENTER].**

The method for adding comments to your configuration files is very simple. You must provide a mark (or *separator*) at the start of each comment line, so that the program reading these files does not confuse comments with actual commands; otherwise, when your operating system tries to run these critical files and execute their commands in sequence, it will either do something you don't wish or perhaps hang up completely.

NOTE You will see that we have used lowercase characters to set off the remarks and comments from the typically uppercase contents of most DOS and Windows files. In this instance, the case is insignificant to the processing of these files, but you should edit commands and options in their original case in any of these files, because many programs are case-sensitive in their interpretation of command lines.

Comments in the CONFIG.SYS File

Prior to DOS version 5.0, there was no provision for comment lines in the **CONFIG.SYS** file. Every line of the **CONFIG.SYS** was read and taken to be a command line. DOS would interpret each line of the file as a command to *configure* your *system* (hence the name **CONFIG.SYS**) and try to run each in turn. Any text that was not a legitimate command caused an error message to appear on the screen as the file was processed at boot-up.

With version 5.0 and above, it is possible to begin a line with the letters 'rem' or 'REM', followed by a blank space, as a marker or separator for comment lines in the **CONFIG.SYS** file. You may also use the *rem* or *REM* marker to disable a command line, to change some way in which your system performs, or while testing the process of making changes to your **CONFIG.SYS** file. These uses for the *rem* statement are commonly called "REMming out" or "commenting out" an active line or "commenting" or "adding a comment" to a file.

A sample **CONFIG.SYS** file with a REMark separator and a comment might appear as follows:

```
DEVICE=C:\DOS\HIMEM.SYS
DEVICE=C:\DOS\EMM386.SYS
DOS=HIGH
rem the following line is used for fancy screen
rem attributes
DEVICE=C:\DOS\ANSI.SYS
BREAK=ON
```

If we want to disable the loading of the **ANSI.SYS** device driver in this **CONFIG.SYS** file, we simply add *rem* as the first characters on the line specifying the device driver, as follows:

```
DEVICE=C:\DOS\HIMEM.SYS
DEVICE=C:\DOS\EMM386.SYS
DOS=HIGH
rem the following line is used for fancy screen
rem attributes
rem DEVICE=C:\DOS\ANSI.SYS
rem above line REMmed out for testing
BREAK=ON
```

Notice that we also added a comment line indicating that the **ANSI.SYS** line was disabled (or "REMmed out") intentionally, and why. Removing the entire line for **ANSI.SYS** would accomplish the same thing, but it would create more work for us if we wanted to reinstall the device driver later, and also fail to tell us or someone else *why* it was removed or disabled, which might be very important.

Comments in the AUTOEXEC.BAT File

The process for the **AUTOEXEC.BAT** file is quite similar to that for the **CONFIG.SYS** file. The *rem statement* simply disables an active command line or prefaces a comment, as shown below:

```
ECHO OFF
CLS
PROMPT $p$g
SET PATH=C:\;C:\DOS;C:\WINDOWS;C:\BAT
CALL C:\BAT\NET.BAT
rem CALL C:\BAT\LOGIN.BAT
MENU
```

In this example, the CALL C:\BAT\LOGIN.BAT is disabled by the *rem* placed in front of it. Do you notice anything missing from this file? The comments, perhaps? Yes! Let's fix that:

```
ECHO OFF
CLS
PROMPT $p$g
SET PATH=C:\;C:\DOS;C:\WINDOWS;C:\BAT
CALL C:\BAT\NET.BAT
rem Disabling the LOGIN since we are taking this
rem system to
rem another office with different network setups.
rem Manually
rem log in instead.
rem CALL C:\BAT\LOGIN.BAT
MENU
```

By substituting a pair of colons (::) for the *rem* characters, you can take advantage of a recently popular shortcut used for comments in **BATch** files (these exceptionally useful files are called **BAT** files for short, since DOS will not allow filenames to have more than three characters as the extension, or the portion after the period). This shortcut can speed up **BAT** file processing and avoid the possible misinterpretation of the contents of rem lines as commands.

As explained in DOS manuals, these BATch files are read, interpreted, and acted upon in sequential, line-by-line order. There are only three types of entries that can appear in the lines of **BATch** files: REMark lines, DOS commands, and *labels*. Labels are short lines of text preceded by a single colon used to identify a grouping of BATch file commands. (The colon or double-colon is valid only in **BAT** files and not the **CONFIG.SYS** file, since labels are indicated by different symbols in **CONFIG.SYS** files, and the **CONFIG.SYS** labels do not work for **BAT** files.)

DOS must spend time interpreting each line, looking for DOS commands to be executed, including those preceded with the rem statement, unless that line is only a label. Label lines are skipped over, so no time is spent interpreting them, and thus label lines can be used instead of rem lines to save time.

To use a label line instead of a *rem* statement, create the label line as an entirely meaningless one, beginning with a pair of colons followed by a blank space (and then your text if commenting). The blank space tends to be a matter of style; it makes it easier to recognize the line as a comment or disabled command line.

This technique also avoids having the line confused with a legitimate working label, and since the colon symbol itself is not a valid label for DOS, it is ignored as a functional label or otherwise.

Our previous example can therefore be changed for faster processing and greater clarity too:

```
ECHO OFF
CLS
PROMPT $p$g
SET PATH=C:\;C:\DOS;C:\WINDOWS;C:\BAT
CALL C:\BAT\NET.BAT
:: Disabling the LOGIN since we are taking this
```

```
:: system to
:: another office with different network setups.
:: Manually
:: log in instead.
:: CALL C:\BAT\LOGIN.BAT
MENU
```

You should use these techniques with all of your **BAT** files in order to properly manage your system configuration.

Comments in Windows Files

Microsoft Windows makes the processes of commenting and of disabling lines in its configuration files a bit easier. All of the typical **.INI** used by Windows programs regard the semicolon (;) as a useless character and skip over lines that begin with it.

A partial **WIN.INI** file with a comment and a command that has been disabled with a comment is shown as follows:

```
[windows]
spooler=yes
load=C:\WINDOWS\SYSTEM\POINTER.EXE
c:\netscape\tcpman.exe
; COMMENT: I won't be using these features this
; week...
; nwpopup.exe c:\sndsys\audcntrl.exe
C:\DVX\dvwinmon.exe
run=
Beep=yes
NullPort=None
BorderWidth=5
CursorBlinkRate=530
```

In this example, one line is disabled—the one loading **NWPOPUP.EXE, AUDCNTRL.EXE,** and **DVWINMON.EXE.** We made the comment obvious above our disabled items, leaving the disabled items intact for replacement later.

WARNING

You should be aware that Windows is limited to reading only the first 32K of your **WIN.INI** and **SYSTEM.INI** files. If these files become too large, by the addition of fonts, features, or your comments, some features may not be available within Windows, or you may not be able to run the Windows **SETUP** program to reconfigure Windows. The solution to this potential problem is to monitor the number of fonts and text and graphics converters, and keep your comments and unneeded lines to a minimum.

Planning Ahead for Changes

By undertaking the discipline of good configuration management, you're in a position to address the questions you need to ask before installing new devices or software:

❖ Are any changes needed/being considered?

❖ Are the changes to improve performance or efficiency?

❖ Do you have enough memory?

❖ Do you have the right CPU?

❖ Do you have enough of the required plug-in or mounting slots?

❖ Will the changes affect other programs or devices?

❖ Are you installing a CD-ROM drive? Sound card? New video card?

❖ If so, are enough I/O addresses and IRQ and DMA assignments available?

With your complete system inventory, outside and in, you'll have these questions answered already; you will be familiar with these requirements when you encounter some of them on the side panels of most software and hardware packages.

This is almost enough information for you to decide that your system can accommodate that new graphics or multimedia program, for example. But what if you need to get set up for multimedia *before* you use that program? Few product packages tell you the configuration information you need to know without opening the box and reading the manual, which most stores frown upon before you buy the product. In addition, knowing what that information means seems just as elusive, unless you have recorded—and understood—your system configuration.

This is where we get to the nuts and bolts, or more appropriately, the switches and jumpers of our system configuration. We will cover these items and what they mean for various devices in the chapters ahead.

Summary

This chapter has been an overview of configuration management and the basic facts and techniques necessary for safe and conflict-free changes. PCs are powerful systems comprised of several interconnected pieces of highly complex high-tech equipment, as well as seemingly magic boxes, and all of these require your attention. We've discussed some of the simple steps you can take toward positive configuration management: to back up the files critical to running your system, to document what's in your system, and to keep track of how it changes over time. By doing so, you leave yourself a way to restore the configuration to its working previous condition if a change should go wrong, and you preserve the information necessary for planning future improvements.

Actively managing the configuration of your system will enable you to identify and resolve existing conflicts, and make system software and hardware upgrades with fewer—we hope *no*—conflicts. As you progress through this book, you'll see how helpful, even necessary, these basic maintenance steps and tools are. We'll cover the use of these tools and the information they can provide us in a subsequent chapter.

CHAPTER 2

LEGACY LIVES ON: The Early Standards We Live With

Topics covered in this chapter:

- ❖ Legacy Devices
- ❖ What Has to Be Configured?
    - ❖ I/O Addresses
    - ❖ Upper Memory Information
    - ❖ IRQ
    - ❖ DMA
    - ❖ Logical Devices

Part of Webster's definition of *legacy* is "something transmitted by or received from an ancestor or predecessor or from the past." We might add the synonymous term *of historical significance.*

As much as we want our PCs eventually to "just know" how to set themselves up and take care of any problems by themselves, we have to face the fact that we are dealing with a distinctly technical situation. The PC was designed by and for engineers—people who were comfortable dealing with haywire prototypes, bare wires, hot soldering irons, and wire clippings all over the floor. That was the state of the technology when the first PC was introduced in 1981. The engineers have based the PC's foundation on the goals, technology, and experience available then. And although we as users no longer have to deal with bare wires and soldering irons, that foundation is the legacy we've been given.

When working with a PC, you are involved with a piece of history. Unless your system is a very early, genuine, original IBM model PC5150 or of similar vintage, you probably don't have to worry too much about it weighing 50 pounds, 5 of which are dust bunnies, 10 of which are the disk drive, another 10 add-in devices, and the rest comprising sheet metal and ceramic-encased chips.

But if you can't wax nostalgic about the good old days, don't fret. You're not missing much; most of it still exists intact, as designed, right there in that sleek 15-pound mini-desktop with the 420M hard disk and 16M of RAM and more computing power than was used to put a crew on the moon. So the box got smaller, lighter, better suited to existing in the family den, and it displays a world of color. It's still a PC and it always will be. Today's PC still starts up looking for the same devices, running the same or similar internal self-checks, trying to boot up its operating system off the same kinds of storage devices, and using memory the same way the original PC did. It just does it faster, and with a few more external complications. Even though we've already put out $3,000 to buy a system and software, we still have to go through certain rites of passage to print out our resumes, Christmas letters, and tax forms.

The PC as it exists may not be playing by *our* idea of fair rules as we would write them if we could start from scratch and design a new machine today, but we have to play by the rules it presents to us. Fortunately, the design team at IBM did impose some good rules, which give some order to the world of PCs. Fortunately, many ingenious people in and out of IBM found some ways to work with, work around, or bend the rules, in our favor. *Un*fortunately, a few *other* equipment designers have broken the rules or tried to make them up as they went along when inventing new PC devices. This has caused us endless days and sleepless nights until we dismissed the renegade devices to the dumpster when we couldn't resolve the conflicts these devices created for us.

After all is said and done, though, 99% of the problems we encounter can be fixed with a little shoulder shrugging, sleeve rolling, and counting to ten with all fingers crossed as we boot up a new attempt at correcting system conflicts.

Our adventure begins with explaining the bare rules as they have existed for many years. This sets the foundation for any and all developments, problems, improvements, and solutions we benefit from today as we go along. The premise here is to become aware of the rules, whether we like them or not, and take advantage of the structure and opportunity they provide us.

Ideally we would address, by example, every possible system conflict that ever existed. Unfortunately, neither you nor I have the time or space for the immense volumes of cases that have been encountered, and surely we'd miss one or two in the process. Instead, as the rules become known in this and the following chapters, they will become clearer, and the pieces will fit into place. We will not be able to work around all of the existing rules—we can't always get what we want—but we can get nearly any PC to live up to the reputation and performance appropriate to the resources at hand.

Thus we enter the legacy of IBM-compatible computing. Our first encounter begins at the beginning—with the original IBM PC, PC/XT, and PC/AT—if only because you've already had enough surprises jumping into the middle of this world.

Legacy Devices

Legacy devices, if not preset or fixed in their configuration as built into the *motherboard* or *system board*, require us to manually set jumpers and switches, usually in accordance with a table of possibly dozens of variations of settings, and in comparison to or contrast with other devices in our PCs. Legacy devices typically do not lend themselves to automatic or software-driven reconfiguration.

Almost all PC devices prior to implementation of the Plug-and-Play standard are considered legacy devices. These include add-in cards and other accessories, and to some extent, the basic PC system itself. Some recent devices may be configured through software settings rather than hardware jumpers, but they may not adhere to the new Plug-and-Play standard. Even *Micro Channel, EISA (Enhanced Industry Standard Architecture)*, and *VESA Local Bus* devices, which provide enhanced configuration and performance features, may fall under the category of legacy devices. *PCI (Peripheral Component Interconnect)* devices have been designed with Plug-and-Play in mind, and most, if not all of them, will meet the PnP standard. PCI devices can also be used in some non-PC systems that support the PCI bus, such as the new PowerPC systems. These require automatic recognition and configurability of hardware devices.

It will become evident and almost tedious to notice how many of the PC devices we have used for years, and still buy and use today, have been influenced by IBM's original design for the PC. In 1981, when the PC was designed, it had 1% or less of the power and expandability it has now, and many fewer options and devices to attach to it. In fact, except for some critical low-level hardware and software constraints and basic functions, today's PC only vaguely resembles the PC of 1981.

Perhaps no other invention has seen so much advancement, proliferation, and acceptance since its introduction as the IBM-compatible PC. Yes, personal computers in general have evolved from a half dozen or so attempts to provide small computers to the average person, yet only two of the original contenders in this market thrive on: the products of Apple Computer, because they were there first, followed by the growth of the IBM PC and its descendants.

For the past several years, while Apple Macintosh users have merely plugged in new disk drives, keyboards, networking features, and document scanners (with multimedia features built into the basic Macintosh system), users of IBM-compatible PCs have struggled with dozens of different hardware and software configurations. We fight minuscule hardware jumpers, illegible labels and switches, converting 1s and 0s to On and Off, and deciphering not just device addresses or identifiers, but IRQ and DMA settings. All because a system designed by and for engineering uses found fame and fortune in the hands of unsuspecting users.

For all the progress we've seen in computer system development, we must still deal with the technical issues of PC system configuration. Even if we invest in a new Plug-and-

Play–compatible PC system, we will probably still use many of our "old" non-PnP devices. Such will be the case for the next two to three years (the typical life of a new piece of hardware) as we replace some or all of our systems and devices with 100% PnP devices.

For those of us still supporting even a small number of older-style PC, XT, and AT systems, legacy is our only option. It may seem easy to say that these systems should be replaced "just because," but several thousand of them abound in businesses, schools, churches, and homes that simply don't need or can't afford newer systems, any more than those of us at the leading edge are willing to part with the investment we just made in our new Pentium system without Plug-and-Play.

In any case, legacy devices present the bulk of the configuration and conflict issues we face in dealing with PCs. The next section addresses the most common types of add-in devices that you could encounter configuration problems with.

What Has to Be Configured?

We usually can't, and probably wouldn't want to alter the extremely low-level internal configurations of our PC system boards. But there are numerous devices we can, and often must deal with throughout the life of any PC system.

Among the frequently added, changed, or removed devices anticipated in the original IBM PC, and subsequently the PC/AT, we typically encounter configurations issues with:

❖ Serial I/O (COM) ports, including internal modems

❖ Parallel I/O (LPT) ports

❖ Video display adapters

❖ Disk drives and adapters

❖ Network interface cards

Subsequent developments provided us with at least two new device types to account for:

❖ SCSI host adapters

❖ Multimedia cards, with and without a CD-ROM interface

All of the devices in our systems require system resources. We can take for granted that each device consumes power and creates heat, and must be cooled by one or two meager fans. In addition, all devices in our PC system consume computer-specific resources other than power and space.

The system resources of concern here may not at first appear to be resources. But I/O addresses, IRQ settings, and DMA channel assignments are indeed computer system resources. They are limited to what is available with your system type, and cannot be expanded by adding more of them. The only "upgrade" step for these resources would be to change from an 8-bit (PC- or XT-class) system to a 16-bit (AT- and higher-class) system.

Because of the way they handle these resources, the legacy devices require the most user or technician attention or intervention during both hardware and software setup processes. In legacy systems, there are a finite number of each of these resources with which we must try to support a myriad of system options. If all of the possible combinations of IRQ and DMA signals and I/O addresses could be used in any way we wanted them to be, we would have approximately 2,000 possible configurations to deal with. As we will see in the next chapter, the number of possibilities is significantly reduced by design and by industry-accepted standards. The most limiting factor is, of course, the least available resource: the number of IRQ signals available to us. This limits us to having only 6 devices active at any one time, even though we may have 10 or 12 devices in our system. But more about this later.

The installation of any new device, or any changes to a device, must be done with the limited availability of these resources in mind, and a knowledge (through the inventory described in Chapter 1) of which resources are being used by other devices.

Addresses Are in Hexadecimal Numbers

Before we tackle the details of IRQ, DMA, and I/O, a few words about the numbers and letters used in computer memory addresses are in order. You will often see the notation and numbering for I/O and memory addresses expressed in *hexadecimal* notation, or *base16* numbering. The design and organization of computers, in 8, 16-, and 32-bit (and larger) increments dictates the use of a non-decimal numbering system. Using a hexadecimal numbering scheme also saves space in memory and on disks. Using this numbering scheme throughout also saves us from having to convert between systems. Comparing the numbering systems simply gives us an idea of scale. Hexadecimal numbers range from 0 (zero) to F, for a total of 16 numerals (0 through 9, followed by A through F). "F" represents the quantity that's expressed as "15" in the *decimal,* or *base 10,* numbering that we're accustomed to using in everyday life; in hexadecimal, if you have "F" of something, you have 15 of them. If you have 10 of something in hexadecimal, you have 16 of them in decimal.

Hex numbers may be indicated by a lowercase letter *h* following simple numbers, or by *0x* preceding more complex numbers, as in 0x3FCD, or, rarely, by a redundant mix of the two, as in 0x3FCDh. If you see a reference to IRQ 14, it's a decimal number and is equal to IRQ Eh. All tables and charts pertaining to IRQ, DMA, and I/O addresses will be in, or can be translated to, hexadecimal.

I/O Addresses

Every hardware device plugged into the I/O slot connectors inside our PCs requires a unique hardware address. During program execution, data and commands are written to or read from these locations.

A PC or XT system affords up to 1 million locations of data storage. AT systems provide up to 16 million such locations, and newer systems provide up to 256 million or more such locations. But not all of these locations are available for hardware devices. In most systems, fewer than 800 address locations are available for I/O devices.

IBM originally defined that specific devices occupy very specific addresses. Some of these devices are internal to the system board or specific to IBM products and uses. Among these, some addresses are reserved, or are to be avoided, because of other system or IBM-specific uses, leaving approximately 25 possible address blocks for the devices, features, and options we may want to put into our PCs. This in a situation where some devices require 4, 8, or even 32 locations each.

Those addresses defined, but not specifically reserved, are used for the common I/O devices that IBM planned for and anticipated in its original system developments. These are the devices we are most familiar with—COM ports, disk drives, and so on. In the progression from the original PC to the PC/AT, a few new devices were added, or the primary address of a major functional device (the hard drive adapter, for example) was changed to accommodate the growth from 8-bit to 16-bit systems and more options.

Tables 2.1 and 2.2 list the specific I/O addressing for PC-, XT-, and AT-class systems. Many of the technical terms in tables are beyond our need to define and understand in the context of configuration management, but we do need to know that *something* is assigned at a given address. This list is compiled from the use of dozens of I/O devices, specifications, and commonly available PC reference material.

TABLE 2.1 *THE ORIGINAL IBM PC AND PC/XT DEVICE ADDRESSES*

I/O Address	System Use or Device
000-00Fh	DMA Controller - Channels 0–3
020h, 021h	Interrupt Controllers
040-043h	System Timers
060h	Keyboard, Aux.
070h, 071h	Real Time Clock/CMOS, NMI Mask
081-083h and 087h	DMA Page Register (0–3)
0F0-0FFh	Math Coprocessor
108-12Fh	Not Assigned; Reserved by/for IBM use
130-13Fh	Not Assigned
140-14Fh	Not Assigned
150-1EFh	Not Assigned; Reserved by/for IBM use
200-207h	Game Port
208-20Bh	Not Assigned
20C-20Dh	Reserved
20E-21Eh	Not Assigned
21Fh	Reserved

220-22Fh	Not Assigned
230-23Fh	Not Assigned
240-247h	Not Assigned
250-277h	Not Assigned
278-27Fh	LPT2: or LPT3: - 3rd Parallel I/O Port
280-2AFh	Not Assigned
2B0-2DFh	Alternative EGA Port
2E1h	GPIB 0
2E2h, 2E3h	Data Acq 0
2E4-2E7h	Not Assigned
2E8-2EFh	COM4:—4th Serial I/O Port
2F8-2FFh	COM2:—2nd Serial I/O Port
300-31Fh	IBM Prototype Card
320-323h	Primary PC/XT Hard Disk Adapter
324-327h	Secondary PC/XT Hard Disk Adapter
328-32Fh	Not Assigned
330h	Not Assigned
340h	Not Assigned
350-35Fh	Not Assigned
360-363h	PC Network Card - low I/O port
364-367h	Reserved
368-36Ah	PC Network Card - high I/O port
36C-36Fh	Reserved
370-377h	Secondary Diskette Drive Adapter
378-37Fh	LPT2: or LPT1:—1st or 2nd Parallel I/O Port
380-389h	Not Assigned
380-38Ch	BISYNC_1 or SDLC_2
390-393h	Cluster Adapter
394-3A9h	Not Assigned
3A0-3ACh	BISYNC_2 or SDLC_1

3B0-3BFh	Monochrome Video Adapter
3BC-3BFh	1st Parallel I/O Port part of mono. video card
3C0-3CFh	EGA Video
3D0-3DFh	CGA Video
3E0-3E7h	Not Assigned
3E8-3EFh	3rd Serial I/O Port
3F0-3F7h	Primary Diskette Drive Adapter
3F8-3FFh	COM1:—1st Serial I/O Port

TABLE 2.2 THE ORIGINAL IBM PC/AT DEVICE ADDRESSES

I/O Address	System Use or Device
000-00Fh	DMA Controller - Channels 0-3
020h, 021h	Interrupt Controllers
040-043h	System Timers
060h	Keyboard, Aux.
070h, 071h	Real Time Clock/CMOS, NMI Mask
081h, 082h, 083h, and 087h	DMA Page Register (0-3)
089h, 08Ah, 08Bh, and 08Fh	DMA Page Register (4-7)
0A0-0A1h	Interrupt Controller 2
0C0-0DEh	DMA Controller Chs. 4-7
0F0-0FFh	Math Coprocessor
108-12Fh	Not Assigned or Reserved
130-13Fh	Not Assigned
140-14Fh	Not Assigned
150-1EFh	Not Assigned or Reserved

170-177h	Secondary PC/AT+ Hard Disk Adapter
1F0-1F7h	Primary PC/AT+ Hard Disk Adapter
200-207h	Game Port
208-20Bh	Not Assigned
20C-20Dh	Reserved
20E-21Eh	Not Assigned
21Fh	Reserved
220-2FFh	Not Assigned
230-23Fh	Not Assigned
240-247h	Not Assigned
250-277h	Not Assigned
278-27Fh	LPT2: or LPT3: —3rd Parallel I/O Port
280-2AFh	Not Assigned
2B0-2DFh	Alt. EGA
2E1h	GPIB 0
2E2h & 2E3h	Data Acq 0
2E4-2E7h	Not Assigned
2E8-2EFh	COM4:4th Serial I/O Port
2F8-2FFh	COM2:—2nd Serial I/O Port
300-31Fh	IBM Prototype Card
320-323h	Not Assigned
324-327h	Not Assigned
328-32Fh	Not Assigned
330h	Not Assigned
340h	Not Assigned
350-35Fh	Not Assigned
360-363h	PC Network Card - low I/O Port
364-367h	Reserved
368-36Ah	PC Network Card - high I/O port
36C-36Fh	Reserved
370-377h	Secondary Diskette Drive Adapter

378-37Fh	LPT1: or LPT2:—1st or 2nd Parallel I/O Port
380-389h	Not Assigned
380-38Ch	BISYNC_1 or SDLC_2
390-393h	Cluster Adapter
394-3A9h	Not Assigned
3A0-3ACh	BISYNC_2 or SDLC_1
3B0-3BFh	Monochrome Video Adapter
3BC-3BFh	1st Parallel I/O Port part of mono. video card
3C0-3CFh	EGA Video
3D0-3DFh	CGA Video
3E0-3E7h	Not Assigned
3E8-3EFh	3rd Serial I/O Port
3F0-3F7h	Primary Diskette Drive Adapter
3F8-3FFh	COM1:—1st Serial I/O Port

When IBM invented its PS/2-series of PC systems, it added a number of internal devices and control ports. Their addresses are provided in Table 2.3 for reference only.

TABLE 2.3 PS/2-SPECIFIC I/O ADDRESSES

I/O Address	System Use or Device
061-06F	System Control Port B (PS/2)
090	Central Arbitration Control Port (PS/2)
091	Card Select Feedback (PS/2)
092	System Control Port A (PS/2)
094	System Board Enable/Setup Register (PS/2)

096	Adapter Enable/Setup Register
100-107	PS/2 Programmable Option Select
3220-3227	COM2:—3rd Micro Channel Serial Port *
3228-322F	COM3:—4th Micro Channel Serial Port *
4220-3227	COM4:—5th Micro Channel Serial Port *
4228-322F	COM5:—6th Micro Channel Serial Port *
5220-3227	COM6:—7th Micro Channel Serial Port *
5228-322F	COM7:—8th Micro Channel Serial Port *

* Micro Channel systems provide an additional I/O data-bus–addressing scheme separate from the I/O bus and addressing of ISA systems. The last six addresses in the table do not apply or compare to non–Micro Channel systems. (See Chapter 3 for more about both Micro Channel and ISA.)

The addresses not planned for or assigned by IBM make up the only address locations that are available to be exploited by new devices. IBM did not and could not anticipate the existence of these devices. New devices not defined by IBM had to squeeze into the few address spaces left. The addresses shown in Table 2.4 are typical of non-IBM add-on devices.

TABLE 2.4 COMMON AFTERMARKET OR NON-IBM DEVICES LISTED BY ADDRESSES USED

I/O Address	System Use or Device
130-14Fh	SCSI Host Adapter
140-15Fh	SCSI Host Adapter (as may be found on a sound card)

220-22Eh	SoundBlaster (SB), SoundBlaster emulation
-or-	
220-23Fh	SCSI Host Adapter
-or-	
228, 289h	AdLib enable/disable decode (port is active if SoundBlaster emulation is available and active)
238, 239h	AdLib enable/disable decode (port is active if SoundBlaster emulation is available and active)
240-24Eh	SoundBlaster; sound cards emulating SoundBlaster
280-283h	Network Interface Card
-or-	
280-288h	Aria Synthesizer
-or-	
280-29Fh	NE1000/NE2000 network adapter
290-298h	Aria Synthesizer
2A0-2A8h	Aria Synthesizer
2B0-2B8h	Aria Synthesizer
300-303h	Network Interface Card
-or-	
300-31Fh	NE1000/NE2000 network adapter
320-321h	MIDI Port
-or-	
320-33Fh	NE1000/NE2000 network adapter
330-331h	MIDI Port

-or-

330-33Fh	SCSI Host Adapter
340-34Fh	SCSI Host Adapter

-or-

340-35Fh	NE1000/NE2000 network adapter
360-363h	Network Interface Card (non-NE-type)

-or-

360-37Fh	NE1000/NE2000 network adapter
388, 389h	AdLib sound device (if no SoundBlaster emulation active)

You'll also want to be able to look up the addresses used by specific types of devices as you add the devices in. Table 2.5 organizes the information that way.

TABLE 2.5 AFTERMARKET DEVICES BY TYPE

I/O Devices	Possible I/O Addresses Used
SCSI Host Adapters	130-14Fh
	140-15Fh
	220-23Fh
	330-34Fh
	340-35Fh
Sound Cards	220-22Eh
	240-24Eh
Aria Synthesizers	280-288h
	290-298h
	2A0-2A8h
	2B0-2B8h

AdLib sound device	228h, 289h
	238h, 239h
	388h, 389h
MIDI Ports	320-321h
	330-331h
Network Interface	280-283h or 280-2FFh
Cards (Note: Novell/	2A0-2A3h or 2A0-2BFh
Eagle (NE) -1000	300-303h or 300-31Fh
and -2000-compatible	320-323h or 320-33Fh
cards consume 20h	340-343h or 340-35Fh
addresses, which can	360-363h or 360-37Fh
easily use up or	
possibly overlap	
other resources.)	

As you can see, there are at least six aftermarket device types (the I/O Devices column) we will frequently encounter. To accommodate these, there are 14 address locations (the Possible Addresses column) available (14 is the number of unique addresses in the table, once repetition is accounted for). Since not all devices provide for being configured to work in any or all 14 of the available addresses, there may still be overlap and conflicts despite the fact that there are more addresses than there are device types. Industry acceptance has limited the addresses that certain devices may use to only a few addresses per device type. Thus, our configuration issues begin.

Upper Memory Information

Not only do we have to consider the few specific low-memory locations available for new devices, but some features and devices require portions of the 384K of memory address space that constitute the upper-memory area between the top end of DOS at

640K and the beginning of *extended memory* at the 1M location. This area provides space for the video BIOS, access to video memory, hard disk BIOS, and system BIOS. Not all of this 384K is used by every system configuration. The original IBM PC, PC/XT, and PC/AT upper-memory assignments are listed in Table 2.6.

TABLE 2.6 *UPPER-MEMORY LOCATIONS FOR VIDEO, DISK, AND SYSTEM BIOS*

Memory Range	System Use or Device
A000-AFFFh	Graphics Video Memory (64K)
B000-B7FFh	Monochrome and Text Video Memory (32K)
B800-BFFFh	Not Assigned *
C000-C7FFh	VGA Video BIOS Location (32K)
C800-CFFFh	Hard Disk Controller BIOS Location (32K) *
C800-CFFFh	Not Assigned *
D000-D7FFh	Not Assigned *
D800-DFFFh	Not Assigned *
E000-EFFFh	IBM ROM BASIC (IBM systems only) *
F000-FFFFh	System BIOS (64K)

* A point of information: Those areas not occupied by a device and not assigned for working video memory are often made available for use as upper-memory blocks (UMBs) by memory managers (such as EMM386, 386Max, or QEMM). This reuse of memory can provide up to 128K of RAM for the loading of device drivers and *memory-resident* programs (such as **MSCDEX, DOSKEY,** and **SMARTDRV**), instead of using lower or DOS RAM for that.

Part of the system boot-up process is to search upper memory for add-in device BIOS code (the addresses in Table 2.7). Any BIOS code found and executed then becomes part of the normal system operation. Hard-drive and SCSI adapters are the most common devices to have their own BIOS on board, which complements or replaces the functions that would otherwise come only from the system BIOS. Table 2.7 lists the commonly available upper memory locations and the types of devices you can or may find configured in them.

TABLE 2.7 *UPPER-MEMORY LOCATIONS THAT MAY BE USED BY THE BIOS IN COMMON I/O AND ADD-IN DEVICES*

BIOS Address	Use
C800-CFFFh	Hard disk controller or SCSI (32K)
C800-CFFFh	SCSI Host Adapter BIOS (32K)
D000-D7FFh	SCSI Host Adapter BIOS (32K)
D800-DFFFh	SCSI Host Adapter BIOS (32K)
E000-E7FFh	SCSI Host Adapter BIOS (32K)
E800-EFFFh	SCSI Host Adapter BIOS (32K)
E000-EFFFh	LIMS EMS Memory Page Frame (64K)

NOTE

The PC system BIOS expects any hard disk controller BIOS (for ST506/412-MFM, RLL, ESDI, or IDE-type disk drive adapters) to be at C800h. IDE and SCSI interfaces cannot occupy the same location. If you have both *IDE (Integrated Drive Electronics)* and *SCSI (Small Computer System Interface)* interfaces in your system, the IDE interface will be fixed at C800h as its default address, and it will always be the primary interface for the hard drives and boot drive (while the SCSI interface will supply only additional hard drives, CD-ROM drives, and so on). Since SCSI host adapters usually have the flexibility to be configured for any one of six upper memory locations, the addressing shouldn't be a problem. If SCSI is the only interface in the system, it can be assigned to any of the even-32K-increment address ranges from C800h to E800h.

IRQ

IRQ, or interrupt request, lines are used by hardware devices to signal the CPU that they need immediate attention and software handling from the CPU. Not all of the devices in your system require an IRQ line, which is good news, because we have only 16 of them (in an AT- or higher-class system). Of those 16, three are dedicated to internal system board functions (the system timer, the keyboard, and a memory parity error signal). The use of the other signals depends on the devices installed in your system and how they should be or are configured.

For ISA or non–EISA, non–Micro Channel systems, it is the general rule that IRQ lines cannot be shared by multiple devices, though with some care and well-written software, they can be. But since there is no easy way to know which devices and software can share IRQ lines with other devices, this is something we will avoid doing. Table 2.8 shows the predefined interrupts that the PC needs.

TABLE 2.8 *IRQ ASSIGNMENTS*

IRQ	PC, XT	AT, 386, 486, Pentium
0	System Timer	System Timer
1	Keyboard Controller	Keyboard Controller
2	Not Assigned	Tied to IRQs 8-15; assigned for older EGA adapters
3	COM2:at 2F8h-2FFh and COM4: at 2E8h-2EFh	COM2: at 2F8h-2FFh and COM4: at 2E8h-2EFh
4	COM1: at 3F8h-3FFh and COM3: at 3E8h-3EFh	COM1: at 3F8h-3FFh and COM3: at 3E8h-3EFh

5	XT HD Controller	LPT2: 378h or 278h
6	Diskette Controller	Diskette Controller
7	LPT1: 3BCh (mono) or 378h (color)	LPT1: 3BCh (mono) or 378h (color)
8	Not Available on PC or XT	Real Time Clock
9	Not Available on PC or XT	Links to and substitutes for IRQ 2
10	Not Available on PC or XT	Not Assigned
11	Not Available on PC or XT	Not Assigned
12	Not Available on PC or XT	PS/2 Mouse port
13	Not Available on PC or XT	NPU (numerical processing unit)
14	Not Available on PC or XT	Primary Hard Disk Adapter
15	Not Available on PC or XT	Not Assigned

The PC and PC/XT provide fewer IRQ resources for expanding these systems. Fortunately, the AT and higher systems have more available IRQ lines for the addition of new devices.

Add-in devices usually provide a number of options for IRQ assignments to avoid conflicting with other devices when installing and configuring them. Some typical IRQ assignment options for add-in devices are shown in Table 2.9.

TABLE 2.9 ADD-IN DEVICE IRQ OPTIONS

Add-In Device Type	IRQ Choices
SCSI Host Adapter	10, 11, 14, or 15
Sound Cards	5, 7, 10, or 11
Network Card	2, 3, 4, 5, 7, 10, or 11

DMA

DMA, or direct memory access, enables a program or device to initiate data transfers between two devices, or between a device and memory, without the intervention of the entire CPU system. It's typically used for high-speed disk operations, multimedia applications, and diskette drive operations.

DMA provides for faster data transfers, since transferring data with the CPU involved takes more time. However, while DMA operations are being performed, all CPU operations are out on hold until the DMA operation completes. (A properly designed DMA application will allow the CPU's operations to execute periodically so that the entire system is not "dead" or at the sole discretion of the DMA process.)

The defined DMA channel assignments are shown in Table 2.10.

TABLE 2.10 *PC, XT, AND AT DMA CHANNEL ASSIGNMENTS*

DMA Channel	PC and XT Use	AT, 386, 486, Pentium Use
0	DRAM Refresh	DRAM Refresh
1	Available/ Not Assigned	Available/ Not Assigned
2	Diskette Controller	Diskette Controller
3	PC/XT HD Controller	Available/ Not Assigned
4	Not Available on PC or XT	Used Internally

5	Not Available on PC or XT	Available/ Not Assigned
6	Not Available on PC or XT	Available/ Not Assigned
7	Not Available on PC or XT	Available/ Not Assigned

There are four DMA channels on PC and XT systems and eight DMA channels on AT- and higher-class systems. Of these, one channel is dedicated to memory refresh operations on all systems. Another is dedicated to the diskette drive system if one is present.

The fact that DMA Channel 1 is the only one available on a PC explains why most sound cards use this channel as their initial default setting.

NOTE

Once again, we see that PC and XT systems provide little room for expansion. The AT and higher systems provide five DMA channels for expansion use, and in a full system with SCSI and multimedia operations, most of these are needed.

The typical DMA channel assignments for add-in devices are shown in Table 2.11.

TABLE 2.11 ADD-IN DEVICE DMA OPTIONS

Add-In Device Types	DMA Choices
SCSI	3 or 5
Sound Card	1, 5, or 7
Network Cards	1, 3, 5, or 7

Logical Devices

Okay, we just want to get our letters and reports out to a printer, *not* to system address 3BCh. Partially for our convenience, to eliminate the complexity of dealing directly with the cold technical details of physical addresses, IBM provides *logical* or "plain-English" translations of the technical complexities of addresses. So we have at our disposal a means to gain access to devices by thinking of their function, rather than having to rewrite or configure each application for the hexadecimal addresses that an individual computer system uses. (Initially, IBM's "logical" translation from the technical nitty-gritty to more digestible terms also facilitated programming in the BASIC language.)

IBM provides for a handful of devices its developers believed we might have use for. These include the COM (serial) and LPT (parallel) ports, which are probably the ones we're concerned with the most often. They also include the disk drives (A:, B:, C:, etc.) and the keyboard and video output (combined as the CON: or system console). Unfortunately, this list of common logical devices has not been expanded on, except to add LPT2:, LPT3:, COM3:, COM4:, and the occasional special hardware and software interfaces that give us other unique COM and LPT devices.

NOTE

In actual use with programs and DOS, these devices must be expressed with their numerical designation followed by a colon (LPT1:, for example, and COM2:), while generically, it's LPT and COM. Specifying only LPT or COM in DOS commands will result in an error message, and the desired command or operation will not occur. For the console and devices of which there is only one of that type, there is no number, such that in conversation you may see "CON" but the computer must use "CON:."

It might be advantageous if we could invent some new devices for the system. Wouldn't it be much easier if we could also refer to and use devices such as a sound card by calling it a new logical device "SND:," or perhaps spell it all the way out as "SOUND:," use "MIC:" or "MIKE:" for a microphone input, "MSE:" or "MOUSE:" for the mouse, "MDM:" or "MODEM:" and perhaps even "PHONE:" for a telephone interface, and so on.

The use of logical device names simplifies things for us in some ways, but ultimately, these "plain-English" devices, services, and resources are still just labels for those physical memory addresses and their attendant internal signals. However, the internal rules that are used to determine where and what these devices are become confusing and seemingly contradictory between the hardware and BIOS in the system, and the applications we use.

NOTE

The logical assignment of parallel I/O, or LPT, ports to specific hardware addresses is not as critical for most applications as is the assignment of serial I/O, or COM, ports. Most software that uses the COM ports works directly with the hardware, bypassing the features built into the system BIOS (because doing so is much faster than using the BIOS features). Because most communications applications access the hardware directly, but make their own assumptions about logical names and physical addresses, the physical and logical device matching, in the order shown in Table 2.12, is expected and critical. Communications applications also require specific matching IRQ assignments to function properly.

Applications that use printers historically haven't dealt with the system BIOS services to access a printer, and may not make use of hardware addresses or interrupts. The more recent development of bi-directional parallel I/O ports, however, makes matching the physical and logical assignments of parallel ports with IRQ assignments essential for intersystem file transfers and obtaining information from new, "smarter" printers.

All of the new operating systems and environments—Microsoft Windows, Windows NT, Windows 95, and IBM OS/2—which strive to fill in where the BIOS and DOS could not in making the hardware easier for us to use, must work on top of the same limited, complex, conflict-threatening foundation we are all dealing with: a PC, its BIOS, and thousands of add-in devices.

Consider Table 2.12, a listing of the most common physical and logical devices encountered in a PC system, to be a foundation set of rules for your system configuration.

TABLE 2.12 *Logical Versus Specific Physical Translations for Common PC Devices*

Logical Device Name	Physical Addresses	Associated IRQ	Function
COM1:	3F8-3FFh	IRQ 4	1st Serial I/O Port
COM2:	2F8-2FFh	IRQ 3	2nd Serial I/O Port
COM3:	3E8-3EFh	IRQ 4	3rd Serial I/O Port
COM4:	2E8-2EFh	IRQ 3	4th Serial I/O Port
LPT1:	3BC-3BFh	IRQ 7	1st Parallel I/O Port (on monochrome systems)
	378-37Fh		(on color systems)
LPT2:	378-37Fh (if LPT1: is at 3BCh	IRQ 7 (change to 5)	2nd Parallel I/O Port (on monochrome systems)
	278-27Fh (if LPT1: is at 378h)	IRQ 5	(278h is the accepted LPT2 device on color systems)
LPT3:	278-27Fh	IRQ 5	2nd or 3rd Parallel I/O Port

NOTE

The issue of logical versus physical devices in a PC is not always an easy one to understand, much less explain. Yet this issue is one of the most significant rule-creating and binding aspects of a PC system, and the root of many conflicts.

The easiest way to deal with this issue is simply to follow the original rules that IBM defined for all of the devices in your system. In fact, that's what is advocated throughout this book: knowing what the rules are and complying with them.

During the *Power-On Self-Test (POST)* when you boot up your system, the system BIOS performs an equipment check, looking for specific devices at specific physical addresses in a specific order. As these devices are found, they are assigned sequential, logical port numbers. BIOS uses this information to control the I/O ports for any application that relies on the system BIOS to provide access to these ports. Thus, when you are working directly with DOS or its applications, such as PRINT, and you send a file to be printed to LPT1:, DOS passes some control over the printing to the system BIOS, and the BIOS "finds" or sends the file to the physical device associated with the "name" of LPT1:.

Where problems originate is in the fact that POST bases its naming strictly on a first-come, first-served basis. Although the logical and physical addresses are matched as shown in Table 2.12, and those addresses are what your system and devices will be looking for during operation, the *actual* order in which these logical devices are assigned may differ. Here's an oversimplified look at the programming logic for finding and assigning COM port labels to serial ports:

❖ POST will look for a communications port first at address 3F8h.

❖ The first serial device that POST finds becomes COM1: If no serial device is found at 3F8 to assign as COM1:, POST continues the search at address 2F8h.

❖ The ports are assigned in the preprogrammed order of 3F8h, 2F8h, 3E8h, then 2E8h.

❖ A port assignment is not "permanent"—if a device addressed "earlier" in this order (before 2F8h, 3E8h, or 2E8h, depending on what already exists) is added, the assignment shifts in order to have COM1: assigned to the first available device in this prescribed order after subsequent bootups.

It does not matter to POST or the system BIOS services if the first serial device POST finds is at 3F8h, 2F8h, 3E8h, or 2E8h. But it matters a lot to your serial communications, since COM ports require properly matching IRQs. It is easier and proper to create a configuration by the given assignments and BIOS rules.

Subsequent logical port assignments are made as devices are found in the search process. If you have physical devices only at addresses 2F8 and 3E8, they become—to your system BIOS, and thus to DOS—logical ports COM1: and COM2:. This is contrary to the rules set forth in Table 2.12 in two ways: First, the hardware address is "wrong," and second, the resulting IRQ assignment is wrong, according to what BIOS and our applications expect. To make matters worse, many serial port cards associate both the address and the IRQ together with each other, such that you may not be able to change the IRQ assignment.

LPT ports are assigned in the same way. The apparent confusion and variable assignments for LPT ports (as noted in Table 2.12) begins with IBM providing a parallel port at 3BCh using IRQ 7 on monochrome display adapters. Any parallel port added to a system had to be at either 378h or 278h. When IBM introduced color systems, any parallel port provided with or added to these was addressed as 378h. Quite possibly this is because you could have both a monochrome display adapter and a color display adapter in the same system, working at the same time. Subsequently, for a color system with an add-in parallel port at 378h, a second port was provided for at 278h.

All three ports can co-exist, though the port at 3BCh and the one at 378h will be forced to share IRQ 7. Since IRQs are not normally used for printing, this did not usually create a problem, but it is in fact a conflict that is tolerated.

If you need a second nonconflicting parallel port, use 3BCh *or* 378h *only* as the first port, using IRQ 7, and add a port at 278h using IRQ 5 for the second port.

NOTE

Always keep in mind that the numeric designation indicates a logical ordering of devices. In order to have a No. 2 or second of something, you must have one or a No. 1 or first "something." You simply cannot reserve or leave gaps in the logical numbering of the devices, as some people have wanted to do. For example, we cannot leave the LPT2: assignment open or "save" it for a possible later expansion of the system by trying to "force" just an LPT1: and an LPT3: existence. BIOS and DOS simply will not allow this to happen.

The same process is used for detecting disk drives, video displays, and so on—but the system BIOS is designed to give us error messages only if there is a problem detecting the memory, keyboard, or video display or if the disk drives aren't properly set up. Since all applications need the console (keyboard and display) and some means of loading the operating system, applications, and stored data (the disk drives), these critical items warrant configuration warning messages. Although most software works directly with hardware devices for communications and printing, IBM's design intended for these functions to be handled by the system's BIOS and DOS services. So IBM didn't think it significant enough to provide error messages if the serial or parallel ports are not properly detected or configured.

For all of the more or less invisible help provided by the BIOS and DOS, neither one of them will tell you what your configuration should be, what conflicts exist, or how to fix them. Windows 95 and OS/2 lack significant detection or help tools in this regard. Windows 95 can tell you what resources are used, but may not clearly indicate which device another conflicts with, and nothing short of opening the case and referring to the equipment manuals will actually *tell* you what the proper IRQ, DMA, or I/O address should be, much less what to do to fix the problem.

Summary

Our emphasis in this section has been to illustrate the basic principles of some common system configuration items. These will be addressed again as we discuss more devices, configurations, and conflicts.

Some of the strongest tools we have to learn from and base solutions on are found in examples of what is, what works, and what doesn't. We have begun our foundation here by outlining the rules of the original PC designs and BIOS. In the next chapter, we'll discuss the interim innovations toward better performance and configurability. Once our foundation is established, we'll look at a variety of typical system configurations. These configurations must work with and around the original PC designs, the new architectures, and the issues of physical and logical devices.

CHAPTER 3

FROM MICRO CHANNEL TO PLUG-AND-PLAY: New Standards, New Solutions

Topics covered in this chapter:

❖ IBM's Micro Channel: System Board and Add-Ins

❖ HP and Compaq's Enhanced Industry Standard Architecture (EISA*): System Board and Add-Ins*

❖ Personal Computer Memory Card Industry Association (PCMCIA): *Additional Data Bus for Portables*

❖ Video Electronics Standards Association's Local Bus (VESA Local Bus, or VL-Bus): *Video I/O Performance*

❖ Intel's Peripheral Component Interconnect (PCI): *I/O Performance*

❖ Generic No-Standards, No-Jumpers, Software-Settable Devices: *Mostly Modems and Network Cards*

❖ Compaq, Phoenix Technologies, Intel Corp. and Microsoft's Plug-and-Play (PnP): *The Solution We've Been Waiting For*

❖ Microsoft's PC95: More than Compatibility

    ❖ Additional Features and Benefits of PC95

        ❖ Energy Conservation

        ❖ On/Off Control in the Keyboard

        ❖ Accessibility

As the PC has "grown up" over time, so have many of its capabilities and complexities. The popularity of PC, XT, and AT systems revealed to the PC industry that higher performance and easier configurability were needed to accommodate the ever-increasing amount of data being used and the resource demands of new applications.

A number of design enhancements have come along to increase performance, configurability, and expandability. We will discuss these items in terms of their contribution toward configuration management and conflict resolution, and in reference to Plug-and-Play as our ultimate hope for no-hassle configurations.

These enhancements include all the ones listed at the beginning of this chapter.

IBM's Micro Channel: System Board and Add-Ins

When IBM introduced its new Micro Channel bus and add-in card design with their new PS/2-series systems, they hoped to improve and reshape the way developers and users dealt with add-in devices. The system board, add-in devices, and methods of configuration changed to a completely different style and format from ISA (Industry Standard Architecture) systems (the PC/XT and PC/AT and compatibles, for which ISA is the de facto standard). Add-in devices designed for PC and AT systems do not fit into Micro Channel systems, and Micro Channel devices cannot be used in ISA systems.

In some ways, this change provides some configuration and performance benefits. In late-model Micro Channel systems, the data or I/O bus expanded from 8 or 16 bits wide to 32 bits wide at faster speeds. Devices contain information within them that can be queried by configuration software. System configuration can still involve the setting of some jumpers and switches, but configuration is otherwise aided (or limited) through the use of a system-specific reference disk that includes a special setup program and resource files that describe the devices in the system.

Another change came into effect with Micro Channel: IBM had previously required that developers license or register their new designs with IBM for inclusion on IBM's reference diskettes. This proved to impede development cycles and gave the impression that IBM wanted to control the market for these systems. IBM has removed many of these restrictions from the development of Micro Channel add-in devices, but the Micro Channel bus architecture is still not very popular or competitive against EISA, Local Bus, or PCI systems.

Because there aren't any non-Micro Channel devices in the system, the configuration program doesn't need to work around the limitations of such devices. It simply finds and guides you to configure Micro Channel devices into a set of configuration rules for the available system resources. The configuration software will provide the user with "pictures" of the devices it knows about and show the preferred settings for any jumpers and switches on the installed devices and those to be added.

The configuration and conflict issues of IRQ, DMA, and I/O addressing still exist, though the configuration software does point these conflicts out and indicates the proper, expected settings for certain devices. The configuration or reference disk software is very helpful in some ways, but the methods are limited to Micro Channel systems only. It does begin to set a target for future configurations and designs to follow. Recently introduced Micro Channel systems will implement the new Plug-and-Play standards for hardware design and configuration.

HP and Compaq's Enhanced Industry Standard Architecture (EISA): *System Board and Add-Ins*

EISA is the result of cooperative design efforts between Hewlett-Packard, Compaq, and other system manufacturers. They, too, recognized the need to make configuration simpler and provide higher-performance systems.

Higher performance is provided in EISA with a full 32-bit data bus and higher bus speeds. EISA devices extend the number and type of bus connections specific to EISA system boards, thus they will not plug into ISA systems. To our benefit, though, EISA does provide compatibility with ISA add-in cards in the same board and socket layout as the new EISA design.

EISA provides several configuration benefits and greater resources through a redesign of how IRQ signals are treated, and by providing more addresses for add-in devices. These features remove some of the restrictions on the sharing of a small number of IRQ lines and fitting devices into a limited range of I/O addresses. But configuring an EISA system still requires handling of jumpers and switches on both EISA and ISA devices installed in the system.

EISA systems use a system-specific EISA Configuration Utility (ECU) program. This program works with special device-specific information files provided by device manufacturers. When you use the configuration program, you can view "pictures" of add-in devices to show you how to set the jumpers and switches.

Once you've gone through the configuration process, the information is saved to the system's internal memory and disk. When you start up the system, the configuration of your system is rechecked against the prior setup, and you are alerted to any changes detected. If you must reconfigure your system, the ECU program lets you select only resources that are available, rather than letting you create a conflict between devices.

Though a slow and tedious process requiring special disks, a lot of device configuration files, and navigation of a complex set of menus, EISA configuration is tremendously powerful. It is not automatic, and it will not in itself solve the classic configuration problems we encounter, but it should work well with Plug-and-Play.

Personal Computer Memory Card Industry Association (PCMCIA): *Additional Data Bus for Portables*

PCMCIA provides an additional data bus scheme to any of the existing data buses we may encounter. It is designed to provide quick, temporary, interchangeable expansion for portable PC systems. Desktop systems may also use PCMCIA devices by installing a PCMCIA adapter. PCMCIA consists of one or more credit-card-sized external data bus sockets for the interconnection of additional memory, software program cartridges, modems, network adapters, and ultra-small hard disk drives with the primary system.

Access to PCMCIA devices requires the use, first, of device drivers that establish the presence of the PCMCIA data bus and sockets to the PC system and, subsequently, device drivers for the device that is connected to the PCMCIA socket.

The use of PCMCIA, and the changing of devices, can require rebooting your system between uses and device choices so that the proper driver software is loaded and does not conflict with other device drivers.

As implemented in most portable systems, PCMCIA should not present any configuration problems to the user, unless two of these devices conflict, which should be rare because the designers of PCMCIA devices work closely together to establish and follow specific configuration rules. There are no hardware switches or jumpers to be set, only device driver software options to set at the time of installation. The device drivers for different PCMCIA devices can conflict with each other, but this is usually resolved by changing the order in which these drivers are specified in the **CONFIG.SYS** file, which determines what order the drivers take effect at bootup.

Video Electronics Standards Association's Local Bus (VESA Local Bus, or VL-Bus): Video I/O Performance

Seeking to expand the display capabilities of PC systems, the Video Electronics Standards Association defined several enhanced video display modes as extensions to the existing *VGA* display modes. In defining these new modes (including Super VGA, or SVGA) which provide better color definition and higher screen resolutions, it was obvious that systems would have to transfer more display information from programs to the display adapter.

PC system performance had to improve, at least the CPU–to–video-display portions of the system. As fast and capable as EISA is, it still could not deliver the performance needed. Out of this need came the Local Bus design, providing a 32-bit-wide data path directly from the CPU to I/O devices, and at CPU data. This new data bus serves to enhance video display speeds as well as providing a faster interface for other devices, most commonly disk drive adapters.

The existence of the Local Bus itself is somewhat invisible to the user as far as device configuration is concerned; the interface chip between the CPU and the bus sockets is aware of whether or not a device occupies a socket, and it handles data and addressing internally. There are typically one to three Local Bus sockets in a Local Bus system. Although Local Bus devices require connection to the ISA bus as well as the Local Bus socket, they do not work when plugged into ISA-only sockets.

The Local Bus in itself does not involve any new or solve any old configuration issues. A Local Bus video card or disk adapter must still present itself to the ISA bus for proper recognition and access, using the same I/O address and IRQ and DMA lines as an ISA device. When the high-speed Local Bus data transfer features are being used, these devices will perform data transfers across the Local Bus to improve performance. The system BIOS and Local Bus controller automatically recognize and handle the shifting of data I/O from the ISA bus to the Local Bus.

Intel's Peripheral Component Interconnect (PCI): *I/O Performance*

In another effort to provide higher I/O performance in PC systems, and to do it closely matched with the original CPU designs, Intel and others designed the PCI bus. PCI exists essentially for the same reasons Local Bus does, and performs much the same service as Local Bus, though using different techniques. Video display, disk drive and network interface adapters are the most common items to benefit from PCI's high performance.

These techniques are such that they can be and have been applied to non-Intel and non-PC systems, such as the Power PC. PCI is completely different from Local Bus in connections and configuration. PCI devices appear to be physically "backwards" from ISA devices, and they use a smaller socket that fits between and apart from ISA sockets. Typically there are one to three PCI sockets on a PCI system board, along with other ISA bus connections. PCI devices maintain compatibility with their ISA counterparts as standard functions as well as PCI devices. The addressing and IRQ issues we have with ISA systems aren't a problem for PCI.

PCI devices are by nature designed to be Plug-and-Play–compatible. PCI device configuration is handled internally through the system BIOS and setup, where addressing and interrupts are assigned by physical socket position. The BIOS does not allow you to configure the system with conflicts at the PCI level.

Generic No-Standards, No-Jumpers, Software-Settable Devices: *Mostly Modems and Network Cards*

Many manufacturers have eliminated the switches and jumpers from I/O cards, and thus eliminated the need to open up the system box to reconfigure a device. This technique has been applied primarily to advanced internal modems and network cards. Intel provides devices in each category. National Semiconductor and various "off-shore," "white box," or no-name manufacturers also provide software-configurable network interface cards.

So far, the Intel products that exist have successfully provided compatibility with prior devices and techniques, and the setup software automatically checks the existing system resources and configuration before indicating possible configuration options for the new device you're installing. This software applies only to the specific device of interest, not to any other device in the system. Plugging in the new card and running the software leaves you with a clear set of safe options for the configuration of that device. If you wish to use a specific configuration, you may have to manually change other parts of your system until the resources you want to use for this new device are available. While this is no help to the rest of your system, it is a very good way to handle the installation of a new device, since it does detect the available resources it can use and helps you set up for this.

Experience with some of the products available from National Semiconductor indicates a similar regard for the existing configuration before allowing configuration for the new device.

Some "no-name" products work in a similarly friendly and successful fashion, while others seem to be designed and implemented without any regard for other possibilities or the existing configuration. The resulting problem can be that they will allow you to create a device conflict during setup. There is also the potential for these devices to mistakenly reconfigure themselves internally, because of poor design, or get in the way of other device detections. These problems can result in system lockups or the device becoming configured to some unknown address or IRQ, so that it will not be available for use as previously expected.

All in all, the basic ISA configuration concerns remain the same with these generic, no-jumpers devices. Whether or not it's done by software configuration, automatically or manually, you have to be aware of what resources are in use and which can be used in your system for various devices.

Compaq, Phoenix Technologies, Intel Corp. and Microsoft's Plug-and-Play (PnP): The Solution We've Been Waiting For

Finally, the no-conflict, no-hassle configuration solution we think we've been waiting for is rapidly headed our way. Compaq, Phoenix Technologies (a primary provider of BIOS for many systems), Microsoft, and Intel spearhead this effort to design cooperative, integrated PC systems, system and add-in boards, and BIOS to work together intelligently.

Plug-and-Play begins at the very basic and lowest level of our PC systems—the system board and BIOS. Both of these must be designed and implemented to work together. The instant we start up a PC system with PnP, this new BIOS, or rather enhancements to existing BIOS, goes to work detecting devices toward automatic configuration of the system. A full and PnP-only system, without legacy devices, will configure and verify itself and make the expected devices and services available to us without much, if any, thought or effort.

Plug-and-Play is designed to work with and around existing legacy devices, whether they are ISA, EISA, Micro Channel, PCMCIA, Local Bus, or PCI. During system startup, PnP's device detection begins to detect any and all system devices and resources. It also determines whether the devices it finds are PnP devices; if not, PnP devices will be configured to use the resources not used by non-PnP devices. If you add a new non-PnP device that conflicts in any way with an existing PnP device, the existing PnP device will be reconfigured at startup to maintain the working status of your system.

Windows 95 has built-in PnP technology to alert you to any changes in your system. Windows 95 will then give you the option of having it reconfigure itself or any PnP hardware so that the system will have access to all of the expected devices and services.

PnP can be *the* answer to configuration and conflict concerns if your system contains only PnP-compatible devices. If any legacy devices exist, as they certainly will for quite some time, you must still follow the existing standard configuration rules when setting up the legacy devices. PnP will not do anything different with or for standard PC port devices, such as the addressing of COM ports, LPT ports, their IRQs, and so on. PnP devices for the most part are still expected to use the originally designed and defined PC configuration standards to work properly with software.

Microsoft's PC95: *More than Compatibility*

PC95 is Microsoft's answer to, or dictate of, what a properly configured and configurable PC system should be by the end of 1995, to work with Windows 95 and similar PnP-compliant operating systems. The PC95 standard is intended to make PCs more affordable, more approachable, and easier to use for non-technical users. This means that there should be no user concerns over I/O addresses, IRQ, DMA, ports, logical devices, etc., and thus no manual configuration when buying or upgrading a PC system.

To fully meet this goal, all hardware devices will have to become Plug-and-Play compatible and be able to be dynamically reconfigured as new devices are added or old ones are removed. This includes all hardware, meaning that even disk drives will also have to support configuration changes (such as first, second, or further drive IDs, SCSI device numbers, and so on). But PC95 is more than compatibility. Windows 95 and PC95 were designed cooperatively, and with the features of Plug-and-Play, VESA (video modes and performance), automatic power management (to serve the U.S. Environmental Protection Agency's Energy Star program for energy conservation in computing devices), and other new PC device standards in mind. Since Plug-and-Play was designed to also be compatible with legacy devices, they are likewise covered under the minimum PC95 requirements. To encourage this, Microsoft is licensing systems as being "Designed for Windows 95," complete with an identifying logo saying so, if they meet certain minimum requirements.

These requirements will be tested by Microsoft's Hardware Compatibility Test for Windows 95. They include CPU type, amount of RAM, video display capabilities, CD-ROM drive performance and capabilities, and multimedia capabilities (sound and video playback). (See Table 3.1.) To date, the Hardware Compatibility Test is not available to the general public, but we can compare its requirements to a variety of system components to see if they might comply.

TABLE 3.1 PC95 SYSTEM REQUIREMENTS

System Components	Minimum Requirements	Recommendations
BIOS	Plug-and-Play BIOS Version 1.0a with resource readback	PnP with soft-set for all resources
CPU	80386 or equiv.	80486DX-33 or equiv.
RAM	4M	8M
Video Adapter	640 x 480 x 256 colors	1024 x 768 x 256 colors
Video Display	640 x 480 color	VESA DDC1/2B standard and Display Power Management Signaling (DPMS) for shutdown
Pointing Device	Dedicated port or integral device	
Parallel Port	Supports compatibility (output only, to printers) and Nibble modes (bi-directional data transfer)	Full IEEE-P1284-I Enhanced Capability Port (ECP) mode compatibility

continued...

continued...

Serial Port	One; two if mouse uses COM port	16550A or compatible serial I/O chip
Hard Disk	Not required if networked	80-120M min.; 500+M recommended
Diskettes	3.5", 1.44M, providing write-protect signal if diskette not present (for disk presence test)	
Sound		22 Khz, 8-bit, mono output only
Labeling	Standardized icons for device plugs for easy identification	
System Board		• Advanced Power Management BIOS interface v1.1; software -controlled power supply power-down
		• High-speed expansion bus (PCI or VL-bus)
General		• CD-ROM drive with soft-eject control
		• SCSI-2 interface

continued...

continued...

- Clearly labeled switches and jumpers on all boards
- Plug-and-Play expansion cards
- Standardized cabling that cannot be plugged into the wrong card or device

The PC95 standard, and in essence the Plug-and-Play standard, will also provide for several more configuration options than we find on standard PC devices. Having more options available provides a great deal more flexibility for adding more devices to our system, though most of the popular and commonly desired items may already be provided with an off-the-shelf PC system.

OTHER REFERENCE

Refer to Chapter 2 for the limitations imposed by legacy devices.

N O T E

If you review Table 3.1 and compare it to your existing system, you may find that except for PnP-BIOS, your system may already be close to meeting the PC95 standard and some of its additional recommendations. If you establish and manage your system's configuration adequately, in essence acting as the plug-and-play manager for your own system, you could at least be "PC94"-compliant without having to replace your system board and other devices.

Additional Features and Benefits of PC95

PnP hardware and software not only address the issues of configurations and avoiding conflicts, they open the door for several new features to be introduced into our PC systems. These new features extend themselves to both usability and environmental issues.

Energy Conservation

A few years ago, energy conservation was simply considered getting more life out of the batteries in laptop systems. On our desktops, the video monitors, the disk drives, and an otherwise idle system are power hogs. They not only use a lot of electricity to run, they also generate a lot of heat, which in most cases we eventually remove with air conditioning. The cumulative effects of several dozen PCs running in an office has overburdened the cooling systems in offices that were designed before PC systems were in common use. Even with new building designs, PC systems can create a waste of facilities energy.

Advanced Power Management in PC systems can be thought of as the ultimate "screen saver" of the '90s. Instead of displaying flying toasters or psychedelic fish, these new features will dim our monitors, stop our disk drives from spinning, and even put the computer system to "sleep" if we leave our systems inactive for a certain period of time. In essence, we will be saving the batteries of the environment.

As to the question of whether it's better to leave your system on or turn it off between uses, as far as *conservation* is concerned, it is better to turn it off. If this feature is designed into the system, the electronic circuits will control the power smoothly, preventing the turn-on/turn-off surges that are suspected in many system failures.

In reality, the PC95 system may not be completely shut off, so that it can come to life again as you need it. Those items that are shut off internally are protected by the power supply regulators, so there is no great in-rush of current through the AC power line as there is when you operate that big red on/off switch on the side.

On/Off Control in the Keyboard

OK, so our friends using Apple Macintoshes will laugh at us for bringing it up, but once we have software control of the power consumption of our system, it's a relatively simple matter to design in the ability to monitor the keyboard periodically to see if anyone's pressed a certain key. This is the way screen savers work already.

Windows 95 is already designed to shut down the system as part of its exit routine from Windows (although it doesn't go to DOS, like before). When you elect to shut down Windows 95, you have several options; one of them is to restart the system (reboot) and the other is to perform a shutdown, at which point Windows 95 instructs you that it's safe to turn your system off.

Eventually the software will be able to shut down the system itself. Since there will be no arm, hand, and fingers provided to toggle the big red switch, the shutdown command will go to an electronically controlled power supply. The big red switch may stay on, but the supply will be turned off inside.

To turn the system back on, we need to get access to that internal electronic control, and since the keyboard is close and used most often by users, it seems like an obvious place to put the On button, just like the Macintosh. OK, so it's not there yet on your PC keyboard, but there's little keeping it from happening.

Accessibility

Windows 95 provides a set of installable options to make the use of a PC system easier for physically impaired users. Currently these options consist of "sticky" keyboard keys, many special one-key operations, large screen characters, and similar items.

The PC95 standard allows for the interconnection of a variety of devices, some yet to be invented, through a Microsoft feature and new standard called the ACCESS.bus. These devices may replace or supplement keyboards and pointing devices with special articulation controls depending on the nature of physical impairment and mobility.

This effort is to be applauded and greatly encouraged throughout the industry, for both hardware and software design. We're all aware of programs that *require* a mouse, if only because a programmer forgot to include the standard set of alternate keyboard commands for a function or designed a new control whose odd new behavior that seems to take forever to get used to.

There are thousands if not millions in the world who would be able to get a lot more out of life, and put a lot more into it, if only they could use these wonderful PC systems. So developers of hardware and software should be encouraged to ensure accessibility.

Summary

This overview of enhancements to the original PC designs should have indicated to you how much things haven't changed, and how much they can and will change toward making PC systems easier for us to set up and use.

Now that we have an initial set of rules to go by, and this recent overview, we can move along and place ourselves into the process of configurations and create our own "plug-and-play" PC systems, complete with informed conflict resolution (your new skills and all of this information) and easy upgradeability.

Chapter 4

WONKING, WARPING, AND WINDOWS: Getting Ready for Those BIG Upgrades

Topics covered in this chapter:

❖ Working with the Rules

❖ General Configuration Precautions

❖ What to Expect from a New Operating System During Installation

   ❖ IBM's OS/2, Version 3.0, a.k.a. Warp

   ❖ Microsoft's Windows 95

❖ What You Can Expect with Hardware Upgrades

❖ Memory Types and Address Ranges

   ❖ An Address Can Represent More than One Memory Location

❖ Lower Memory

  ❖ Hardware I/O Area

❖ Upper Memory

  ❖ Expanded Memory (LIMS-EMS)

  ❖ BIOS Addresses

❖ Extended Memory

  ❖ High Memory

❖ Virtual Memory

❖ Please Excuse the Interruption

  ❖ Making the Best Use of IRQ Selections

❖ Upgrading a Typical "Clean" 386/486/Pentium Configuration

  ❖ Out of the Box

  ❖ Getting Ready to Upgrade

    ❖ Using Multiple COM Ports

A *wonk* is one of those computer gurus who is able to make everything work just right. A wonk's system is finely tuned, maybe constantly being tuned to perfection. *Wonking* is getting your system up to speed in the most efficient manner possible, and keeping it there.

Warp is IBM's name for OS/2 Version 3.0. If you're Warping, the chances are you've wonked. If you'll be switching to Windows 95, you'll want to wonk as well. If you'll be upgrading your hardware, you'll be into some serious wonking.

When you consider any upgrade project, especially one as significant for you and your system as a new operating system or a major hardware addition, you should make every effort to ensure that your system is configured properly *before* performing the upgrade. This will help ensure that the upgrade goes smoothly and quickly so you can begin to enjoy it rather than regret it. Of course, this is no different from the advantages of having your system configured properly in the first place, but if you've waited until now to deal with the issue, you may as well deal with it all the way.

This chapter is applicable before performing any upgrade, including the following:

Operating Systems:

❖ Changing to IBM's OS/2 Warp

❖ Changing to Microsoft's Windows 95

❖ Changing to Microsoft's Windows for Workgroups

❖ Changing to Microsoft's Windows NT

Multimedia:

❖ Adding a sound card

❖ Adding a video capture card

❖ Adding a CD-ROM drive

Networking:

❖ Adding a local area network card

❖ Adding a high-speed modem or a fax/modem

Storage Devices:

❖ Changing from IDE to SCSI hard drives

❖ Changing from SCSI (Small Computer System Interface) to IDE (Integrated Drive Electronics) hard drives

❖ Mixing IDE and SCSI hard drives

Somewhere in one of these upgrade processes, some device may be found to conflict with another device; a port will be found to be improperly addressed; a logical device will not be available or it will not function as you expect it to. If you're lucky, the installation program for your new sound or network card will help you through the configuration details. Operating system upgrades are considerably more complex because they must work with all of the devices in your system.

If you're not so lucky, you may be able to get through an upgrade process but, having finished the installation of OS/2, for example, you add the NetWare for OS/2 drivers, restart the system to enable the network drivers, and suddenly, *nothing*. You encounter a system error message and the system is frozen.

Or you're clicking around in a fresh installation of Windows 95 trying to find your system settings, and you decide to add a new network protocol in the Add New Hardware Wizard. In checking your hardware, the Help dialog appears, telling you, "Device conflicts with another in your system..." What will you do?

You could fight these conflicts for an hour or so and then call another expert, call technical support, or, worse yet, simply back out of the process, uninstall the upgrade, try it again, or give up and keep using DOS and Windows "the old-fashioned way." Instead of the frustration, within a few minutes, perhaps 30 at the most, you could determine your configuration, correct any problems, and begin enjoying the new upgrade much sooner and happier.

Working with the Rules

OTHER REFERENCE

In Chapter 2, we discussed the hardware, BIOS, and DOS design "rules" for PCs. If you have not yet read and followed through with the system inventory and configuration records portions of this chapters, *stop now, go back,* and do some basic configuration management homework. You will be *very* glad that you did! Having accomplished those steps, you will find the items covered later in this chapter easier to understand and implement.

The rules or design of PC systems could not and did not anticipate the number, variety, and complexity of the devices that have been invented to plug into a PC, even though this may seem a bit odd for a system that was designed by and for engineers. It took many other engineers only a few years to work around the existing rules and fit new devices into the holes and gaps that were left available in the IRQ, DMA, and I/O design.

The challenges were significant. Engineers designing new hardware had to hope that IBM would not overshadow any new work and try to force major new devices into the PC standard that IBM established. Fortunately for us and several hundred hardware and software companies, IBM—perhaps not knowing what to do with the PC after it was introduced—decided to leave the market and new designs to flourish on their own.

Since the release of the IBM PC to the marketplace, we have seen dozens of innovations that have allowed us to be more productive and comfortable with the PC, and we have been able to enjoy it a lot more. Some of these innovations have come from IBM, and many have come from third-party or aftermarket sources. Not all of them were introduced for the PC initially, but made their way to the PC market as users and investors saw their potential. Among these are innovations and their originators are:

❖ Monochrome graphics (Hercules)

❖ Color graphics (IBM)

❖ Enhanced color graphics (IBM)

❖ 16-bit data and processing in the i80286 CPU (Intel)

❖ 32-bit data and processing in the i80386, i80486, and Pentium CPUs (Intel)

❖ High-resolution color display (VGA)

❖ Enhanced VGA display (VESA)

❖ Networking (Novell and others)

❖ Memory expansions and enhancements (Lotus-Intel-Microsoft and others)

❖ SCSI, (an ANSI standard)

❖ Pointing devices (Xerox)

❖ Graphical user interfaces (Xerox)

❖ High-speed modems (Hayes and others)

❖ High-capacity/high-performance disk drives (Shugart, Seagate)

❖ CD-ROM drives (Sony)

❖ Sound and music interfaces (Creative Labs)

- ❖ High-performance I/O interfaces
  - ❖ EISA (COMPAQ, Hewlett-Packard)
  - ❖ VESA Local Bus (Video Electronics Standards Association)
  - ❖ PCI (Intel)
- ❖ Real-time video capture and playback (various)
- ❖ High-performance and multiple-processor systems (Intel's Pentium)

To fit all of this into a system with relatively limited expansion options, considering the original PC design, is indeed amazing. Yet we are here, doing it and enjoying it. Combining and progressing through these features over the years has been tremendously exciting for millions of people. It has caused a great many of us to learn new things and provided untold opportunities for users, designers, programmers, content providers, and the like.

The existing rules have added to the original rules, and just when we think we've run out of room, ideas, and resources, something else comes along to extend the life of what began as essentially a "smart" data terminal.

In the process of upgrading our system's hardware and software, we are going to work with all of the rules and enhancements that IBM and others have provided for us. We will see some limitations and have to make some judgment calls based on available resources, the hardware we have at hand, the hardware we want to add, and our overall needs. We will also expand on I/O addressing as it relates to the memory types in your system.

NOTE

As we go along, it should not come as too much of a surprise that it may be more efficient to invest in a second PC system, dividing the type of work to be done between systems configured specifically for one type of application and hardware or the other. For instance, one system may be set up with several modems or a mix of modems and network cards to handle telecommunications, while another system could be set up for multimedia production work with scanners, CD-ROM drives, and printers. You would share data between the two systems as a small peer-to-peer network.

If an application works best under one operating system or the other, but this differs from the other applications to be used, configuring to be able to switch operating systems at bootup may also be considered. If information needs to be shared among systems, networking and the attendant configuration issues with that upgrade is another consideration. This is part of the planning and configuration management process, as well: evaluating the type of work you do, what you do it with, and what system configuration will get it done best.

General Configuration Considerations

Most of the precautions in this book apply to all system configurations, but some have special significance for new operating systems and most hardware upgrades. When setting up your system, either to establish an initial configuration or to change devices with an upgrade or replacement, there are any number of known and often unknown limitations we could face. Some of these are the obvious limitations of which I/O addresses and IRQ and DMA channels an add-in device or its software will let us use.

Add-in devices don't always allow complete freedom of choice for their configuration options. Some devices provide a list of fixed options, locking certain addresses, IRQs, and DMAs together without any flexibility. You might find this circumstance with cards that provide only a few jumpers or switches to set only a few predetermined options that the card has made available.

Similarly, not all software allows complete and flexible configuration of the ports, IRQs, and DMA channels it will support. Investigate carefully how configurable a software package is before buying. Many stores will let you view the software on a demo system, allowing you to check out the setup and other features of the package.

Generally speaking, operating system upgrades and use are quite possible and successful. Large companies (Microsoft and IBM) have invested a great deal of time and money in making their products succeed, and to do so, the products have to be readily installable.

If you can reconfigure other devices in your system around any limitations your new hardware may present, you'll be OK. If not, consider buying a more flexible add-in device—one that lets you set any configurable item independent of the others.

What to Expect from a New Operating System During Installation

For the past couple of years, software marketing departments, the press, and users have been anticipating the direction towards which users would turn for a higher-performance operating system and interface environment. The old 8-bit DOS we've been using since 1981 has been enhanced by a variety of utilities and user interfaces, from the Norton Utilities to Microsoft Windows to Quarterdeck's DESQview/X, but none of these interim improvements has really been able to take full advantage of 32-bit processors, data buses, and just plain speed in getting data from one place to another.

All of the DOS add-ons to date have had to maintain a firm grasp on compatibility with the DOS file systems and other system- and software-related I/O functions so that the same software and files could be shared with older, slower 8- and 16-bit PCs. Since you can't buy a new 8- or 16-bit PC anymore, and we demand higher performance in display, data transfer and program execution speeds, the only choice is to make a full-scale transition of operating systems to make use of the power and speed available in 32-bit PC systems.

Users have also come to expect that systems be easier to set up, easier to use, and easier to fix or upgrade. As you might expect, easier should also apply to our pocketbooks. Since we users are paying for these things we should be able to enjoy greater productivity with less cost, and now our demands are finally being met.

We've had access to the Unix operating system for years. Unix is very powerful and works on more types of computers than any other operating system, but it is also very costly and complex to implement and use. There are many very attractive and effective graphical user interfaces for Unix, but they, too, are costly and complex. Even though Unix is almost universal across various systems, it has never been designed, packaged, or supported for use by the general public. Yet we've wanted to be able to use something with the high-performance, multitasking, interconnection features of an operating system like Unix.

At one time, Microsoft and IBM were co-developing the operating system that became OS/2. Due to a variety of competitive and business differences, Microsoft left OS/2 for IBM to develop by itself while Microsoft pursued a higher-performance variation of Windows, which became known as

"NT," for "new technology." Thus the user market already struggling with the differences in system performance, and the tentative shift to using Windows, had to wait a little longer for Windows NT and/or OS/2 to come on the market and compete.

Windows NT gained popularity and was implemented before OS/2 and on a larger number of user systems, in very special, limited environments. Versions of NT were also developed for systems other than PC-compatibles, such as the PowerPC, as a power-user's operating system. OS/2 made it to market and stuttered along mostly in IBM-supported corporate environments until version 2.0 was stable enough for power users (wonks) to buy and try. Even though IBM, with its OS/2, made it to market first with a 32-bit operating system that users could afford and work with easily, the majority of PC users have a significant investment in Windows and have decided to wait for the next move by Microsoft.

By the time Microsoft gave us our first glimpses of test versions of what we heard would be "Windows 4.0" or "DOS 7" or "Chicago," and has finally become "Windows 95," IBM had put enough polish and support behind OS/2 upgrades to release version 3.0 as the first 32-bit operating system for the average user. Many of us are enjoying full-time use of OS/2 while running side-by-side comparison tests with Windows 95. There are some tremendous similarities in the two systems' improvements in ease of installation, use, and performance versus DOS and Windows. As well, these two new operating systems share certain system configuration requirements and precautions before they can be beneficial to the general user market. Indeed, this is what the next few sections are intended to cover—preparation and optimization of your system configuration for the new 32-bit operating systems and some generic upgrades.

IBM's OS/2, Version 3.0, a.k.a. "Warp"

Not to give IBM's impressive new operating system a bad name, but OS/2 Warp is incredibly unforgiving if the system hardware and configuration details are not set up properly. The cryptic, numbered error messages you might receive are unfriendly, poorly documented, and generally not the least bit helpful to you in terms of correcting problems.

Warp comes with a System Information Tool, but this is not normally installed unless you select it at installation time. Then, if you can't get the new operating system to run in the first place, you can't get to the software tools that might be able to help you solve the problem.

If you have a problem with Warp, go back to DOS, check your configuration, correct any problems found so that your system has no IRQ, DMA, or address conflicts, and start over. An easy Warp installation can take up to an hour of your time if all goes well. A problem-ridden Warp installation may never succeed, consuming entire evenings or days if you let it.

Microsoft's Windows 95

Microsoft's Windows 95 is impressive and almost fun to experience, even during the installation process. However, it too may consume an hour of your time, or a day if things don't go well because of a bad system configuration.

What You Can Expect with Hardware Upgrades

As often as it's possible to make just about any combination of PC hardware devices work together, there are cases where two devices are just not compatible in the same system. This is usually because one or both devices lack flexibility in their configuration options, or because the software for one device or the other is equally inflexible or just poorly written.

You will find more compatibility problems with older hardware and software (designed when only the PC, XT, or AT systems existed) than you will with products designed after 80386 systems came along. The latter are faster and take into account more memory addressing and management considerations. Not only were the electronic components used in I/O devices and system boards prior to the 80386 slower than today's components, but the methods used by some manufacturers to address their I/O devices led to conflicts with 16-bit and 32-bit systems. This consideration, the use of older, and likely slower, I/O devices applies mainly to moving older COM and LPT ports, memory cards, and non-SCSI or non-IDE disk controllers for older-style disk drives into faster 386, 486, and Pentium systems. Some of these older devices may work, but at the cost of limited performance or possible configuration conflicts.

If you have decided to upgrade several items, you should add or upgrade only one feature or component at a time. This will prevent you from creating conflicts, ensure that each new device functions properly with your present system, and avoid any confusion that could be caused by trying to deal with multiple configuration issues at the same time.

You may even find it beneficial to test each individual upgrade item separately, by not leaving another in place, to be sure each item works with your system. Then add each consecutive item back until all of them are in place and working together.

If you have a Plug-and-Play system, and are adding a Plug-and-Play upgrade item, save this upgrade for last in a multiple-upgrade situation. This will allow the PnP item to configure itself around the non-PnP items.

Memory Types and Address Ranges

Addressing and memory present certain connotations and expectations in terms of your system configuration. There are several significant address ranges, regions, areas, or types of memory in your PC system. By "type," we aren't referring to the electronic or technical details of the components involved (such as RAM, ROM, CMOS, FLASH, dynamic, or static) but to the typical contents and uses for the memory and its addressing in our systems relative to devices and their configuration. Discussion of these areas and their differences is also important for operating system setup, memory management, and their use as system resources for application programs.

The areas of memory you will encounter with your system configuration are:

❖ Base memory or DOS memory, including lower memory
❖ Upper memory, including expanded (LIMS-EMS) memory and BIOS addresses
❖ Extended memory, including high memory
❖ Virtual memory or swap space

Memory areas can be represented or expressed without a comprehensive study of computer memory, but those that are pertinent in the context of this book are shown in Table 4.1.

Of these memory types, in the context of hardware configuration management and conflict resolution, only the base memory and upper memory areas are of concern and are discussed in depth here. For specifics about your system memory or memory management software, consult the documentation for your system, operating system, and software.

TABLE 4.1. MEMORY ADDRESSING AREAS

Memory Area	Address Range	Amount
Base or DOS memory	0:0000-9:FFFFh	640K
• Lower memory	0:000-0:A00h	64K (within base memory)
• System Internal I/O	0:000-0:100h	256 bytes (within lower memory)
• Hardware I/O	0:100-0:3FFh	768 bytes (within lower memory)
• BIOS data area	0:400-0:4FFh	256 bytes (within lower memory)
• DOS data area	0:500-0:5FFh	256 bytes (within lower memory)
• DOS	0:600-0:A00h	
• Program and data area	0:A00-9:FFFFh	576K
Upper memory	A:0000F:FFFFh	384K
• Graphics memory	A:0000-A:FFFFh	64K (within upper memory)
• Text display memory	B:0000-B:FFFFh	64K (within upper memory)
• Video BIOS	C:0000-C:7FFFh	32K (within upper memory)

continued...

continued...

• Hard drive BIOS	C:8000-C:FFFFh	32K (within upper memory)
• LIMS-EMS expanded memory	E:0000-E:FFFFh	64K (within upper memory; see text under "Upper Memory")
• System BIOS	F:0000-F:FFFFh	64K (within upper memory)
Extended memory	from 10:0000h	At least 256M
• High memory	10:0000-10:FFFFh	64K (within extended memory)
Virtual memory/ swap space	Depends on configuration	Limited to available free disk space

NOTE

The variety of memory addresses shown in the tables in this chapter are expressed in what is called *segment:offset* notation. This notation makes expressing and calculating a wide range of addresses much easier to organize for programmers and hardware designers, and, to some extent, easier for us as well: The numbers aren't as "big" or as hard to do arithmetic on. Each address includes two numeric ranges; the first is the hexadecimal number for the *segment*, representing a 64K block of memory. The second is the hexadecimal number for the *offset*, the location within—and relative to the start of—the specified segment. Thus, address 0:0h is the first byte in the first 64K of memory, and C:8000h is 8000h bytes from the bottom of the thirteenth 64k segment (since hexadecimal numbering starts with 0 and Ch equals 12 in the decimal system). Segment Ch starts at 768K from the first byte of memory.

By convention, since the addresses for I/O devices are in the lowest, or "0," segment, the segment notation is left off of I/O device addresses in most places, so the abbreviated 378h is really 0:0378h in segment:offset notation. Similarly, when we are dealing within a single area of memory, such as upper memory, it has been common to combine the segment and the offset together for brevity, thus where you may see C800-CFFFh, the segment:offset notation is really C:8000-C:FFFFh. The abbreviated notation is how these addresses typically appear in the documentation for various devices. It is not necessarily incorrect, just seemingly less complicated.

An Address Can Represent More than One Memory Location

As you refer to the PC, XT, and AT device-addressing tables shown here and in Chapter 2, you may notice that some devices use a range of addresses starting at a given single location. I/O ports, using the serial port address for COM1: as an example, are typically known by a single address, in the case of COM1: it would be 3F8h. This address is what is called the *base I/O address*, but the port really uses a range of addresses from 3F8h to 3FFh, or eight memory locations. This is because each memory location represents a different portion or function of the serial port—one for data sent to the port, one for control information, and so on.

This issue also pertains to the BIOS addresses for many I/O devices, as the BIOS requires a wider range of address "space" and can usually be configured for a variety of different locations within upper memory, as we'll discuss later.

For most add-in devices and all standard devices, such as COM ports, we know by design and published standards which addresses and how much address space is "mapped out" for a particular device. You will see very few cases in hardware I/O address tables where a standard I/O device is designed to allow addressing overlap, but this does happen.

SPECIFIC DEVICE

One of the most common and little-known cases of potential addressing overlap can occur with a common network interface card, the NE1000- and NE2000-compatible cards. These cards use more than the standard four addresses mapped out for the IBM PC network card (360 to 363h), actually mapping out 20h, or 32 full memory locations, from 360 to 37Fh for data and control information.

You'll see that placing an NE1000- or NE2000-type network card at address 360h will cause the network interface card to overlap the default address for an LPT port at 378h. If you have trouble staying logged onto your network while printing, or you have trouble printing while connected to your network, this is a good place to start looking. Change the network card's address to something else (280h, 2A0h, 320h, or 340h are generally good alternatives.)

Lower Memory

We have primarily been concerned with I/O device addressing in what is called the *lower memory* region of the PC system. This region is a 64K part of the greater region of memory called the *system base memory* or *DOS memory*, which encompasses 640K of memory addressing. Within lower memory are stored a variety of system parameters and some parts of the BIOS enhancements and the operating system that are placed there during the system bootup process.

System information software may look at the BIOS and DOS data areas to report on certain logical devices, the state of the keyboard, types of disk drives, and other tidbits critical to the function of the system BIOS and DOS. What we do as part of system configuration affects the information that ends up in these areas.

Hardware I/O Area

In terms of system hardware addressing, we are concerned with a very small range of addresses: the hardware I/O range from 100h to 3FFh. Within this area, based on design and current uses, we have approximately 20 usable hardware addresses within which we can configure our I/O devices.

Anytime there is activity between the CPU and I/O devices, some portion of this memory area is addressed in order to gain access to the hardware, control it, and exchange data with it.

Upper Memory

Upper memory occupies 384K of memory range between the base or lower memory area ending at 640K and 1024K (1M). There is, by design, no actual system memory in this area. In terms of total system memory (base or DOS RAM plus extended memory), this area is skipped over and not used or filled in with RAM. Any system memory greater than 640K begins at 1024K. Except in some very rare and unusual cases which 99.9% of us will never encounter, no I/O devices are addressed here, either. Within this area are specific blocks for specific system functions—the video display or the system BIOS or the BIOS for some of the I/O devices.

This region is exploited by a feature, often called *shadowing*, that is either built into some systems' BIOS program or is provided by memory management software programs. Without going into a lot of technical details, the components that store the system BIOS and any hardware BIOS are many times slower than system memory. By copying, or "shadowing," the contents of the BIOS chips into faster system memory chips, many system functions work much faster. Shadowing is implemented in some system BIOS programs and may be controlled in the system setup screens. In addition to or instead of shadowing, memory management software such as DOS's EMM386 and Quarterdeck's QEMM perform these enhancements with software loaded when you start your system.

These software programs may also make it possible to use some portions of upper memory for storing and running device drivers and other resident software, including parts of DOS. This is a feature known as *loading programs high* (placing them into upper memory blocks, or UMBs). These drivers and other resident programs would otherwise consume base memory, leaving less memory for applications programs and their data. By loading programs into upper memory blocks, and in some cases also redirecting some of the extended memory into empty upper memory space, EMM386 and QEMM make more base memory available, such that we can have a full 640K of DOS memory for applications software.

Expanded Memory (LIMS-EMS)

Within upper memory, there may be 64K configured as the access to *expanded memory*—memory conforming to the Lotus/Intel/Microsoft–Expanded Memory Specification (*LIMS-EMS*). LIMS-EMS is a special type of memory conceived and designed to provide additional memory for a variety of applications for PC and XT systems that did not have the capability for more than 640K of memory. EMS or expanded memory requires special device-driver software (EMM386,

QEMM, and the like) and, prior to the 80386 systems, also required special add-in memory cards.

This newly designed memory area was intended for the data created and used by large applications such as the spreadsheet program Lotus 1-2-3. This memory type, and how it is handled, also provided more manageable and useful memory than the extended memory that became available with AT systems (IBM called this "expansion memory"). Later versions of LIMS-EMS also made possible the first implementations of multitasking and program swapping before the 80386 systems became available. Today EMS is still useful and available for data storage, disk caching, and loading programs high. It does not bear any special system configuration concerns in this book's context.

BIOS Addresses

The BIOS for most devices requires 32K or 64K of upper memory. The beginning address for the device BIOS must typically start at a 16K, 32K, or 64K address increment, although some devices may allow the beginning of the BIOS address to be set in increments as fine as 4K or 8K. A listing of typical and recommended BIOS addresses for certain devices is given in Table 4.2.

TABLE 4.2. EXPECTED AND OPTIONAL BIOS ADDRESSES

Device	Expected BIOS Address	Optional BIOS Addresses
Video Card BIOS	C:0000-C:7FFFh	None
XT and AT Hard Disk BIOS	C:8000-C:FFFFh	None (unless SCSI)

SCSI Host Adapter	None	C:8000-C:FFFFh
		D:0000-D:7FFFh
		D:8000-D:FFFFh
		E:0000-E:7FFFh
Network Adapter Boot ROM	None	C:8000-C:FFFFh
		D:0000-D:7FFFh
		D:8000-D:FFFFh
		E:0000-E:7FFFh
LIMS-EMS Memory Page (see Note below)	None	D:0000-D:FFFFh
		E:0000-E:FFFFh
IBM ROM-BASIC	E:0000-E:FFFFh	None
System BIOS	F:0000-F:FFFFh	None

NOTE

If you use the enhanced features of memory management products such as Quarterdeck's QEMM program, the 64K LIMS-EMS memory page frame may occupy any available and continuous 64K address range in upper memory. This is due to special memory handling techniques unique to these products, the discussion of which is handled extremely well in their respective documentation.

The issue of address overlap can be a problem with the BIOS for certain I/O devices just as it can be with certain hardware I/O addresses. As with hardware I/O addresses, to avoid conflicts you should find documentation pertaining to the amount of BIOS address space the device may need. Some devices may require only 32K for the actual BIOS program, but in fact occupy a full 64K of address space. This is a critical consideration if you have multiple devices that require BIOS address space. You must be able configure all of the devices' BIOS to fit into the limited number of address segments that are available without having their total required space overlap into the space required by another device's BIOS.

Extended Memory

Extended memory became available with the introduction of the PC/AT system and the additional addressing capabilities of this 16-bit system. AT-class systems based on the 80286 CPU could address up to 16M of RAM.

With the first megabyte of RAM occupied by the 640K of DOS or conventional memory and the 384K of upper memory, 15M of RAM was left for programs to store the data they worked with. This memory area could also be used for creating virtual disk drives or RAM disks, being assigned a logical disk drive designation and able to "fool" DOS and other programs into using RAM as a very fast disk drive. Extended memory is also a common place to reserve memory for use in disk *caching* (storing frequently used data as it passes between the system and a disk drive), or printer caching (holding data on its way to the printer) to improve system performance.

Until MS-DOS 5.0 was released, use of extended memory was limited, because neither DOS nor other programs had a cooperative way to manage the use of extended memory. DOS 5.0 provided the **HIMEM.SYS** device driver, to be loaded at system startup through the **CONFIG.SYS** file, which provided extended memory with better control via an enhancement called *XMS*, the Extended Memory Specification. With XMS, program developers could reliably use extended memory and began to enhance their programs to use XMS instead of EMS (expanded memory). Since extended memory exists as part of the system hardware, rather than being created and managed by a device driver such as EMM386 creates expanded memory, it can be accessed faster and provides higher performance than does EMS.

High Memory

High memory is a 64K portion of extended memory, just above the upper memory area, into which DOS can load one program or set of data, instead of placing that program or data into the lower or base memory. This area is created and controlled by the **HIMEM.SYS** device driver or a similar memory management program. Typically, it is occupied by a portion of DOS itself, when you use the DOS=HIGH command line entry in the **CONFIG.SYS** file.

Virtual Memory

Virtual memory or *swap space* is actually a file on your disk drive. The contents of this file changes as you change applications. The operating system or environment, such as Windows, shifts the contents of RAM in or out of this file so that the program you are working with has more of the faster RAM to work with. This type of memory is not included in normal memory or I/O addressing.

Please Excuse the Interruption

The PC's CPU accommodates only one hardware interrupt input to let it know that something needs its attention. Because of this, the IRQ signals from I/O devices are sent first to a component on the system board known as the *interrupt controller*. This component handles up to eight possible interrupt signals, providing for IRQ 0 through 7. It also assigns a priority (or "who's most important") to the interrupt signals it receives. Priority is given to the lower-numbered IRQs. The system clock is given the highest priority, using IRQ 0, to keep the computer's "pulse" going, and the keyboard is given the second-highest priority, using IRQ 1, so you can get the computer's attention.

Only one interrupt controller is present on the 8-bit IBM PC- and XT- compatible systems. It's responsible for sending all of the hardware interrupt information it receives to the CPU. It also sends, when the CPU "asks" for it, the identification of which IRQ line generated the interrupt activity.

AT-compatible (16- and 32-bit) systems contain two interrupt controllers, with the second one handling IRQs 8 through 15. Since the CPU provides only one connection for one interrupt controller to signal the CPU, the interrupt signal from the second component is connected to the IRQ 2 input of the first interrupt controller. Since IRQ 2 receives the next highest priority after the clock and keyboard, and it gets input from the second component's IRQs 8 through 15, these higher-numbered IRQs actually receive higher priority than the lower-numbered IRQs 3 through 7.

The interrupt controller is designed to allow a number of them to be connected end to end to work together in this fashion.

Making the Best Use of IRQ Selections

High-speed communications programs, working with modems making connections between two PC systems, will perform better if they are on COM2: using IRQ 3 (or on COM4: using IRQ 3, but not at the same time that COM2: is being used) because IRQ 3 gets a relatively high priority.

At connection speeds of 9600 bps or higher, even with the benefits of using the popular 16550 UAR/T (serial port) chip, it is recommended that you give high-speed communications all the priority and CPU time you can to avoid loss of data as it is transmitted, received, and handled by your communications software.

WARNING

Because COM ports are logical devices, preassigned by the system BIOS to physical serial ports and IRQs, you should not try to change the IRQ settings of COM ports to an available higher-priority IRQ line (9 to 15) unless you can and want to reconfigure your software for this type of configuration. Windows does provide for this reconfiguration, but it is unusual and often overlooked, such that it could make support difficult later on. (See Chapter 2 for an explanation of logical devices and how they're assigned.)

N O T E

Also in the realm of high-speed communications and IRQ priorities, configuring 16-bit network cards for either IRQ 9 or 10 will ensure efficient network communications since networks operate much faster than serial ports.

Similarly, if you are doing high-quality/high-speed multimedia work, you may wish to configure your sound or video capture card for a higher-priority IRQ if the card and its software provide for this configuration.

Upgrading a Typical "Clean" 386/486/Pentium Configuration

Now we'll look at two system configurations, covering the most available and obvious aspects of system configuration: one before we add in new features and options, and another that includes "everything" you might find in a fully equipped, networked, multimedia PC.

Our jumping right into a 386, 486, or Pentium configuration does not necessarily ignore the many PC, XT, and AT systems that are still in use. The rules applied to and primary resources available on a PC (8088-CPU-based system) and an 80486- or Pentium-based system are fundamentally the same, except that a 286, 386, 486, or Pentium system provide more IRQ and DMA channels. Likewise, many of the problems and problem-solving processes are the same for all types of PC systems. However, because of the earlier systems' limitations, it's unlikely or impossible that these systems will be considered as upgrade candidates for the types of software and hardware with which we will encounter problems today.

For our purposes, we must take for granted in our example many of the built-in items and some unusual low-level system configuration items that are in use and can't be changed. These include the system's keyboard, memory, and clock circuits.

Out of the Box

Most new PC systems sold today come equipped with the basic features and software that we will need to get started in computing. These include display, data storage, some facility for a mouse or pointing device, and access to communications features. These are provided with common I/O ports and default settings that work in almost every system for most of the common applications software. If you buy a complete new system, these features are expected to exist and work properly. A typical configuration you could expect to see is listed in Table 4.3.

TABLE 4.3. A TYPICAL BASIC SYSTEM CONFIGURATION

Device	Address	IRQ	DMA	BIOS Location
Serial port/ COM1:	3F8h	4	N/A	N/A
Serial port/ COM2:	2F8h	3	N/A	N/A
Parallel port/ LPT1:	378h	7	N/A	N/A
Diskette drives	3F0h	6	2	N/A
Hard drive (IDE)	1F0h	14	N/A	C:8000-C:FFFFh
				(32K)
PS/2-Mouse port	64h	12	N/A	N/A
VGA video	3B0-3BBh and 3C0-3DFh		N/A	C:0000-C7FFFh (32K)
Internal use (BIOS)	No hardware address	0, 1	0, 4	F:0000-F:FFFFh (64K)
NPU (if present)	No hardware address	13	N/A	N/A

Based on the resource allocations listed in Chapter 2, this basic configuration leaves us quite a few system resources available for expansion, as shown in Table 4.4.

TABLE 4.4. SYSTEM RESOURCES AVAILABLE FOR EXPANSION USE

Resource Type	Resource
Addresses	130h, 140h, 280h, 2A0h, 300h, 320h, 330h, 340h, 360h

| IRQs | 2, 5, 9, 10, 11, 12, 15 |
| DMA Channels | 1, 3, 5, 6, 7 |

SPECIFIC DEVICE

In more than one case, accepting a common default network card I/O address of 300h has been known to cause problems with installations of, or changes to, OS/2 and Windows 95. This address is specified by IBM to be for a "prototype card." Even though the address range at 300h has a full 20h locations (300-31Fh) mapped out for it, OS/2 and Windows 95 don't always "like" this location in some systems. The best solution appears to be to set the network card for an adequate and clear address range, such as 280h, 2A0h, 320h, or 340h.

Getting Ready to Upgrade

The lure of virtual travel to exotic places, new electronic-mail pen pals, and the sights and sounds of innovative World Wide Web pages and exciting multimedia CD-ROMs can be resisted no longer. We've decided to upgrade, and we're going to do it all at once, since we'll have the covers off and the wires exposed.

Hmmm, inside this system doesn't look like it's going to provide us with a scenic coastal drove; it's more like an endless, narrow, twisty mountain road, or some 14-car freeway pile-up. Still, we'll drive on and see where this search for adventure takes us.

We'll start with the configuration of some common devices as they are taken out of their boxes. The first step is to list the system resources these devices are set up to use before we fiddle with installation programs, switches, and jumpers. If we upgrade this system by installing as many new devices as we can think of, our configuration might begin to look like Table 4.5.

TABLE 4.5. THE DEFAULT CONFIGURATION FOR COMMON
UPGRADE DEVICES

Device	Address	IRQ	DMA	BIOS Location
Serial port/COM3:	3E8h	4		
Serial port/COM4:	2E8h	3		
Parallel port/LPT2:	278h	5		
SCSI adapter	330h	11	5	D:8000-D:FFFFh (32K)
Sound card	220h	5	1	
MIDI port	388h			
Network card	300h	3	3	

If we overlay Table 4.5 with the details of the original
configuration, we will begin to see some conflicts, as shown in
Table 4.6.

TABLE 4.6. THE UPGRADED CONFIGURATION BEFORE
RESOLVING CONFLICTS

Device	Address	IRQ	DMA	BIOS Location
Serial port/COM1:	3F8h	4		
Serial port/COM2:	2F8h	3		
Serial port/COM3:	3E8h	4		
Serial port/COM4:	2E8h	3		
Parallel port/LPT1:	378h	7		
Parallel port/LPT2:	278h	5		
Diskette drives	3F0h	6	2	
Hard drive (IDE)	1F0h	14		C:8000-C:FFFFh (32K)
PS/2-Mouse port	64h	12		

VGA video				C:000-C:7FFFh (32K)
SCSI adapter	330h	11	5	D:8000-D:FFFFh (32K)
Sound card	220h	5	1	
MIDI port	388h			
Network card	300h	3	3	
Internal to system		0, 1	0, 2, 4	F:0000-F:FFFFh (64K)
Reserved (NPU)		13		

After a quick review, two conflicts should be quite obvious: LPT2: and the sound card are both set up for IRQ 5; and COM4: is trying to share IRQ 3 with the network card. Deciding which device gets to keep its assignment and which one must change is first determined by knowing what the rules are. Then resolving these conflicts is relatively easy.

As we have seen earlier in this chapter, IRQ 3 is designed to be assigned to both COM2: and COM4:. While this can be a conflict in itself, we must first adhere to the original standard. This means that the COM port retains the IRQ 3 assignment and the network card must be given a new assignment.

Which IRQ we assign to the network card depends a great deal on how many different ways we can configure this card. If it is a 16-bit network card that provides the options of using IRQ 2, 3, 4, 5, 7, 9, 10, or 11, we should opt for one of the other available IRQ settings. Obviously it should not be 4, 5, 7, or 11 because the COM ports, LPT ports, sound card, and SCSI host adapter are already using these. The obvious choice for a fully configurable network card seems to be IRQ 10. If the card is an 8-bit card, usually only IRQs 2, 3, 4, or 5 would be available, so IRQ 2 would be the only choice, so far.

But there is more to consider in this choice. In a 16-bit system, IRQ 2 receives all of the interrupt activity from the second interrupt controller, and it is recommended that a device that would normally use IRQ 2 be moved instead to IRQ 9. Since you can't get access to IRQ 9 with an 8-bit card (the connection is simply not there), IRQ 2 will have to be assigned to and "share" any use of IRQ 9 if your applications can properly discriminate between which hardware uses IRQ 2 and which uses IRQ 9. The only way you'll know may be to set up the configuration using both IRQs, use the software for the devices that use IRQs 2 and 9, and see if any problems arise. If either of the applications does not work properly, you will have to reconfigure one of the devices to use a different IRQ. This is one case where some configurations that should be allowed are not adequately supported by application programs, and the detection and resolution of such problems is by trial and error. Of course, we're trying to prevent trial-and-error configuration processes, and can very often do so. In the end, IRQ 10 is still the preferable setting for the network card, if it's available.

Going on, we'll resolve the IRQ 5 issue between the LPT2: port and the sound card. There is a little-known consideration to bring up at this point: Most applications that support LPT port functions (printing) do not have any provision for IRQ operations. Those that do use IRQs during print operations would be said to provide interrupt-driven printer handling—for example, the remote print server application (RPRINTER) for Novell NetWare and the interrupt-driven printing option for OS/2 Warp. (Unlike earlier versions of OS/2, Warp requires an IRQ for LPT port functions only if you have added the /IRQ option to the DEVICE=PRINT01.SYS line in your OS/2 **CONFIG.SYS** file.)

With the rarity of interrupt-driven printing in mind, we could keep the sound card on IRQ 5 and move on. However, there are other uses for the parallel port to consider: applications such as Traveling Software's LapLink which provide high-speed system-to-system file transfer features, network adapters or external SCSI host adapters. Programs that use the parallel port with these options may need the IRQ signal intended for the parallel (LPT) port. You may also have to assign a DMA channel for some applications that use an enhanced parallel port.

We'd prefer a really "clean" system configuration so we don't encounter problems later on. Like the network card example, if the sound card is a 16-bit device, it should allow us access to IRQ lines 2, 9, 10, and 11, and possibly others, but most allow only the choice of 2, 5, or 7. Since IRQs 5 and 7 are assigned to LPT ports, we should use IRQ 2.

We'll reconfigure the sound card to use either IRQ 2 or IRQ 9, depending on if the card provides switch or jumper access to either of these lines. The resulting configuration appears in Table 4.7.

TABLE 4.7. THE UPGRADED CONFIGURATION AFTER RESOLVING CONFLICTS

Device	Address	IRQ	DMA	BIOS Location
Serial port/COM1:	3F8h	4		
Serial port/COM2:	2F8h	3		
Serial port/COM3:	3E8h	4		
Serial port/COM4:	2E8h	3		
Parallel port/LPT1:	378h	7		
Parallel port/LPT2:	278h	5		
Diskette drives	3F0h	6	2	
Hard drive (IDE)	1F0h	14		C:8000-C:FFFFh (32K)
PS/2-Mouse port	64h	12		

VGA video				C:0000-C:7FFFFh (32K)
SCSI adapter	330h	11	5	D:8000-D:FFFFh (32K)
Sound card	220h	9	1	
MIDI port	388h			
Network card	280h	10	3	
Internal to system		0, 1	0, 2, 4	F:0000-F:FFFFh (64K)
Reserved (NPU)		13		

Well, this new upgraded configuration looks pretty good. Everything has a proper, legal, unique assignment—or does it? What about the COM ports sharing IRQs 3 and 4? Is there *any* way to resolve this potential problem?

In most cases, not all of the COM ports are used at the same time. If we have, in the past, used some COM ports at the same time we were using other COM ports, we've probably encountered some lockups, slow performance, scrambled e-mail messages on screen, or loss of data. Typically, if you have a mouse or other pointing device that uses a serial port, it is connected to COM1:.

Using Multiple COM Ports

You may have a need to use COM3: or COM4: at the same time you're using COM1: or COM2:. This situation will normally create an IRQ conflict between COM1: and COM3: or between COM2: and COM4:, since they "share" IRQs.

A workaround might be to take advantage of the possibility that the LPT ports may not need to use the IRQs assigned to them. (DOS and Windows don't; OS/2 and a Novell network server provide the option to do so.) This would give us IRQs 5 and 7 to work with. This will work only if the software to be used with COM3: and COM4: can be reconfigured to allow the use of IRQs 5 and 7 respectively, and the I/O device provides switch or jumper settings so you can set the device for either of these nonstandard (for COM ports) IRQs.

If you need to use two COM ports, your mouse is on either COM1: or COM2;, and you have a PS/2-style mouse connection on your system, change your mouse to one with a PS/2-style connection to free up the COM port you are using now. Some pointing devices come with or can use a special adapter cable to convert them from a serial port connection to a PS/2-style connection.

There aren't many easy options for using multiple COM ports no matter how you look at it. Usually something in the configuration has to "give," either in hardware or in software.

Summary

This chapter has taken on a lot of diverse topics in an attempt to put the PC configuration rules and upgrade concerns into the integrated perspective of a typical hardware upgrade.

What we've discussed should serve as a model for the many considerations that are encountered with most typical systems. It is unlikely that too many systems will differ from our example. Many systems will benefit significantly by duplicating our configuration as shown.

To take a different approach to demonstrating how to follow the rules and implement them in a typical system, the next chapter covers examples of resolving some of the most common conflicts.

CHAPTER 5

TOP TEN CONFLICT AREAS AND HOW TO DEAL WITH THEM

Topics covered in this chapter:

- ❖ Number 1: IRQ Signals
- ❖ Number 2: DMA Channels
- ❖ Number 3: I/O Addresses
- ❖ Number 4: OS/2 Warp or Windows 95 Won't Complete Installation or Run with a Network
- ❖ Number 5: Coincident Printer Port and Network Card Problems
- ❖ Number 6: Coincident Network Card and SCSI Host Adapter Problems
- ❖ Number 7: There's No Sound, the Sound Card Output Stutters, or Voices Sound Like the Computer Took a Deep Breath of Helium

❖ Number 8: Windows **SETUP** Indicates Not Enough Memory to Run **SETUP**

❖ Number 9: Windowed DOS Applications Appear Fuzzy, or Colors Are Changed Between Windows and Windows DOS Sessions

❖ Number 10: But I Really Need to Use More than Two COM Ports at One Time...

❖ Bonus Points

In this chapter, we will be discussing some of the most common questions and conflicts encountered with PC system configurations and providing some quick solutions. Some of the items will be straightforward: "If *this,* do *that."* Some of the items will be a little more anecdotal.

If you've rushed right into this chapter from the front cover, you may find it more beneficial to take the time to at least look over Chapters 1, 2, and 4, which provide a lot of helpful introduction, background, and reference information that lead up to the direct conflict resolution we'll be encountering here. If you've gone through all of the chapters, you'll recognize many of these items from the in-depth coverage already given them, but they're worth highlighting here because they are frequently encountered conflict problems. Without further delay....

Number 1: IRQ Signals

Taking each IRQ line one at a time in a summary format, we'll break them down into the devices that might be configured on them, where the most conflicts seem to be, and what seems to work best in most cases. (See Table 2.8 for IRQ information in table format.)

IRQ 0: Assigned to and used internally for system timing. The IRQ 0 signal line is never available to add-in cards. It is connected only to the internal system board circuits. If a conflict appears to arise with this IRQ, as indicated by system information software, the chances are that your system board is bad.

IRQ 1: Assigned to and used internally for the keyboard. The IRQ 1 signal line is never available to add-in cards. It is connected only to the internal system board circuits. If a conflict appears to arise with this IRQ as indicated by system information software, the chances are that your system board is bad.

IRQ 2: Assigned for older EGA video adapters. This IRQ line is typically available unless one of your application programs needs this line connected on your video adapter for backward compatibility with the older EGA video functions. With most of us having VGA video adapters and displays, this IRQ typically has no primary, useful assignment and can be used for other devices. If another device needs or uses IRQ 2, make sure that the jumper or switch for this IRQ is disabled on your video card. This is a good alternative IRQ option setting for sound or network card use. Because IRQ 9 uses IRQ 2 to communicate with the CPU, you should be aware that there may be a conflict with a device on IRQ 9 if your software for either of the devices using IRQ 2 or IRQ 9 can't determine which device caused the IRQ activity, but most can.

IRQ 3: Primarily assigned to COM2: (at 2F8h) and COM4: (at 2E8h). Unless your system is misconfigured and you've got crossed port assignments with COM1: or COM3:, or you are trying to use devices on COM2: and COM4: at the same time, there are few conflicts if this IRQ is used for COM2: and COM4: only. Sound cards, serial I/O (COM) ports, modems, network cards, and possibly other devices offer this IRQ configuration option. Many network cards come preset to use IRQ 3 when you buy them. Avoid IRQ 3 for the network card if you use serial port COM2: or COM4:.

IRQ 4: Primarily assigned to COM1: (at 3F8h) and COM3: (at 3E8h). Unless your system is misconfigured and you've got crossed port assignments with COM2: or COM4:, or you are trying to use devices on COM1: and COM3: at the same time, there are few conflicts if this IRQ is used for COM1: and COM3: only. Sound cards, serial I/O (COM) ports, modems, network cards, and possibly other devices offer this IRQ configuration option.

IRQ 5: Primarily assigned to the second parallel port (at address 278h). Sound cards, serial I/O (COM) ports, modems, network cards, and possibly other devices offer this IRQ configuration option. Normally you would reserve this IRQ for LPT2: use, unless you need to use it for another device and you are aware that you may have to give up any interrupt-driven printing operations for a second LPT port.

IRQ 6: Assigned to the diskette drive system and is available to add-in cards through the add-in card slots. If you have diskette drives in your system, do not set any other devices for IRQ 6. Few if any I/O cards let you assign anything here anyway, so there should be no conflicts.

IRQ 7: Usually assigned to the first parallel port (at address 3BCh or 378h.) Sound cards, serial I/O (COM) ports, modems, network cards, and possibly other devices offer this IRQ configuration option. Normally you would reserve this IRQ for LPT1: use, unless you need to use it for another device and you are aware that you may have to give up any interrupt-driven (requiring the IRQ signal) printing operations for the first LPT port. If you need two printer ports, don't set them for 3BCh and 378h. Leave one at either of these two addresses, and configure the second printer for address 278h and IRQ5.

IRQ 8: Reserved for the internal real-time clock for AT- and higher-class systems. The IRQ 8 signal line is never available to add-in cards. It is connected only to the internal system board circuits. If a conflict with this IRQ appears in one of the system information programs, the chances are that your system board is bad.

IRQ 9: Another common IRQ option for 16-bit network cards. If you have a sound card and can't set it to IRQ 9, put the network card here. Remember, this IRQ also equates to IRQ 2, so it will get a high priority during use. If high-speed network performance is your priority, set the network for this IRQ and use another IRQ for less critical devices.

IRQ 10: A common IRQ option for 16-bit network cards. This is a safe bet unless you have other devices set for this IRQ. Check the IRQ setting of your sound card if you suspect conflicts here.

IRQ 11: A common IRQ option for many SCSI host adapters and 16-bit network interface cards. Few if any conflicts exist using this option unless you have multiple SCSI host adapters, multiple network cards, a mix of SCSI and network cards, or some other device(s) set for IRQ 11. If you already have a SCSI host adapter set for IRQ 11, try using IRQ 10 for the network card.

IRQ 12: Used for the PS/2-style mouse port (also known as the internal, or on-board, mouse port) included on many system boards. If this port is enabled in your system setup and you are using a PS/2-style mouse plugged into this port on the system board, don't set any other adapters or devices for this IRQ. IRQ 12 is commonly one of the IRQ setting options for SCSI host adapters and sound cards, which you can't use if you're using the on-board PS/2-style mouse port on IRQ 12.

IRQ 13: Reserved for the NPU (a.k.a, math chip, numeric coprocessor, or floating-point processor). The IRQ 13 signal line is never available to add-in cards. It is connected only to an NPU or CPU socket. If a conflict with this IRQ appears in one of the system information programs, the chances are that your system board is bad.

IRQ 14: Assigned to hard drive adapter/controllers for AT systems, and a common optional IRQ setting for some SCSI host adapters. If you are using the hard drive interface built into your system board, or if you have an add-in–card disk drive adapter, *and* you have or are adding a SCSI host adapter or any other add-in device, do not set the SCSI host adapter or any other add-in devices for IRQ 14.

IRQ 15: A common IRQ option for many SCSI host adapters—few if any conflicts will exist with other devices. But if you have multiple host adapters, they cannot be set for the same IRQ, so IRQs 9, 10, and 11 would be likely next choices.

Number 2: DMA Channels

As with the IRQ signals above, we'll be taking each DMA line one at a time in a summary format. We'll break them down into the devices that might be configured on them, where the most conflicts seem to be, and what seems to work best in most cases. Remember that DMA lines may be separated on your add-in cards into DRQ (DMA request) and DACK (DMA acknowledgment) signals, which must be configured to the same-numbered channel for the add-in device to work correctly.

DMA 0: Assigned internally to the system board for memory refresh. You shouldn't be able to even get at it.

DMA 1: Has no predetermined assignment. It's a common choice for sound cards and SCSI host adapters.

DMA 2: Assigned to the diskette subsystem. If you have no diskette drives, you may configure here anything that offers this line as an option, but there are several others to choose from.

DMA 3: Has no predetermined assignment. It's a common choice for sound cards and network interface cards.

DMA 4: Linked to DMA 0-3. Generally not available.

DMA 5: Has no predetermined assignment. It's a common choice for sound cards and SCSI host adapters.

DMA 6: Has no predetermined assignment. It's available for various uses.

DMA 7: Has no predetermined assignment. It's a common choice for sound card use.

Number 3: I/O Addresses

130h: A common alternative for SCSI host adapters.

140h: A common alternative for SCSI host adapters.

220h: Typically used for Sound Blaster or Sound Blaster emulations on sound cards.

240h: An alternative selection for Sound Blaster or Sound Blaster emulations on sound cards.

278h: Assigned to LPT2: or LPT3: and goes with IRQ 5.

280h: One of the typical choices for your network card or Aria Synthesizer.

2A0h: Another common choice for your network card or Aria Synthesizer.

2E8h: Assigned to COM4: and goes with IRQ 3.

2F8h: Assigned to COM2: and goes with IRQ 3.

300h: A common but not ideal choice for a network card. Avoid it for OS/2 and Windows 95.

320h: A good place for a network card if you don't have a SCSI or MIDI adapter at 330h.

330h: A common place for many SCSI host adapters.

340h: A common alternative for many SCSI host adapters, or it's a good place for your network card if you don't have a SCSI host adapter here.

360h: If you need to put your network card here, put LPT1: at 3BCh, not 378h, or the network card may conflict with the LPT port at 378h.

378h: The assignment for LPT1: in color systems; goes with IRQ 7. Beware of an IRQ conflict if you have an LPT port at 3BCh.

3BCh: LPT1: in monochrome systems; goes with IRQ 7. Beware of an RQ conflict if you have an LPT port at 378h.

3E8h: Assigned to COM3:, which goes with IRQ 4.

3F8h: Assigned to COM1:, the first or only COM port you may have. It goes with IRQ 4.

Number 4: OS/2 Warp or Windows 95 Won't Complete Installation or Run with a Network

In OS/2, networking features are an option that has to be added to an existing OS/2 installation, even if your system was networked before you installed OS/2. The installation of networking is not a complex process, and typically it proceeds rather smoothly. Networking is not available until after the installation of the add-in software and device drivers, and a shutdown and restart of the operating system. It's during the restart of the operating system that you may encounter a system error message such as SINGLE01 or SYS3175, which will be your first indication of a possible configuration conflict between your network card and OS/2.

For Windows 95, the installation and configuration of networking are an automatic part of the installation process if a network interface card is detected. Although the process may detect the network hardware and appear to configure Windows 95 correctly, you may discover that networking simply does not work after installation. This may be indicated by the lack of a Network Neighborhood icon on the Windows 95 desktop, or network configuration problems.

If you encounter network problems such as these, check the hardware address for your network interface card. If the card is set up at address 300h, change the address to 280h or 340h. To avoid conflicts with any present or future SCSI host adapter cards at 330h, do not use address 320h, and to avoid conflicts with a present or future parallel port card at 378h, do not use address 360h.

Reconfiguration of a network card may also require editing any and all of the **NET.CFG** files that are part of your particular network configuration. Normally the **NET.CFG** file may be found in the root directory of your boot drive. For Windows 95, you must also change the resources configuration under the Windows 95 Network or System icons within the Control Panel under the My Computer icon to reflect the new network card address.

Number 5: Coincident Printer Port and Network Problems

If you're experiencing problems staying "connected" or logged in to your network server when you print a document on a local printer, or if you're having problems printing locally while working with files on your network, check the addresses used by your network interface card and your printer port.

If you have an NE1000, NE2000, or compatible network interface card that's set up to use address 360h and your local printer port is set up at address 378h, you have an overlap of address space. NE1000, NE2000, and compatible network cards require a full 32 (20h) address locations, including their base address of 360h. Address 378h of the parallel I/O port card falls at the 25th address location required by the network card.

The solution is to change the address assignment of one of these devices. You have three addressing options for the parallel I/O port—3BCh, 378h, and 278h. Most network interface cards provide at least six addressing options: 280h, 2A0h, 300h, 320h, 340h, and 360h.

Since most of us have color video display systems rather than monochrome (text-only or Hercules monochrome graphics), using display cards with parallel ports included on them, and the LPT1: port for these systems is generally accepted to use address 378h, it is probably best to reconfigure the network interface card to use another address. The best alternatives are often 280h or 340h, to avoid further conflicts, since 300h may cause problems with OS/2 Warp or Windows 95 and 320h will overlap the common SCSI host adapter address of 330h.

Reconfiguration of a network card may also require editing any and all of the **NET.CFG** files that are part of your particular network configuration. Normally the **NET.CFG** file may be found in the root directory of your boot drive. For Windows 95, you must also change the resources configuration under the Windows 95 Network or System icons within the Control Panel under the My Computer icon to reflect the new network card address.

Number 6: Coincident Network Card and SCSI Host Adapter Problems

If you're experiencing problems with your SCSI-interface CD-ROM or disk drive when working with files on your network, or if you're having trouble staying connected or logged in to your network server when you access your disk drives, check the addresses used by your network interface card and your printer port.

If you have an NE1000, NE2000, or compatible network interface card that is set up to use address 320h and your SCSI host adapter is set up at address 330h, you have an overlap of address space. As expressed before, NE1000, NE2000, and compatible network cards require a full 32 (20h) address locations, including their base address. Address 330h of the SCSI host adapter card falls at the 17th address location required by the network card, whose base address in this case is 320h.

The solution is to change the address assignment of one of these devices. Depending on the requirements and design of your SCSI host adapter, you may not have any addressing options other than 330h. Since most network interface cards provide at least six addressing options (280h, 2A0h, 300h, 320h, 340h, and 360h), it's probably best to reconfigure the network interface card to use another address. The best alternatives are often 280h and 340h. They avoid further conflicts, since 300h may cause problems with OS/2 Warp or Windows 95 and 360h will overlap the parallel port address of 378h.

Reconfiguration of a network card may also require editing any and all of the **NET.CFG** files that are part of your particular network configuration. Normally the **NET.CFG** file may be found in the root directory of your boot drive. For Windows 95, you must also change the resources configuration under the

Windows 95 Network or System icons within the Control Panel under the My Computer icon to reflect the new network card address.

Number 7: There's No Sound, the Sound Card Output Stutters, or Voices Sound Like Your Computer Took a Deep Breath of Helium

Your sound card requires three distinct, nonconflicting system resources—an IRQ line, a DMA channel, and a hardware I/O address. If the physical configuration of your sound card does not match the settings for the card in your Windows **SYSTEM.INI** file, or if there is an IRQ or DMA conflict with another device in your system, the sound card will not function properly. If you can't correct these symptoms through the methods indicated here, the sound card may be defective.

Most sound cards can be configured without conflicts to use address 220h or 240h, IRQ 5, and DMA channel 1 or 3. Common conflicts may be with a SCSI host adapter that uses address 220h or 240h. Begin solving these symptoms by using a system-information reporting program to determine what resources are used and, indirectly, which resources are available for your sound card configuration. Make any necessary configuration changes to the hardware to suit the available resources, and then use the sound card's installation or setup program to view the existing sound card configuration to be sure it is correct and works with the program designed for the card. In most cases, the configuration details may also be viewed and edited directly within the Windows **SYSTEM.INI** file.

Examples of driver configuration entries in the Windows **SYSTEM.INI** file for five different popular sound cards are provided below. Make sure the entries in your file match the actual physical configuration of your sound card.

Creative Labs Sound Blaster, Old Driver Version

```
[sndblst.drv]
port=220 ("port" means the I/O address here, and
the hex address is implied)
int=5 ("int" stands for "interrupt," or the
hardware IRQ, here)
dmachannel=1
Palette=
MasterVolume=10, 10
FmVolume=8, 8
CDVolume=8, 8
LineVolume=8, 8
VoiceVolume=8, 8
```

Creative Labs Sound Blaster, New Driver Version

```
[sndblst2.drv]
port=220
int=5
dma=1
```

Aria Synthesizer

```
[aria.drv]
dspport=0x2b0 ("port" means the I/O address here)
dspirq=12
midiport=0x330
midiirq=9
```

```
savemix=1
recsource=1
extmon=0
CDmon=0
extmode=0
CDmode=0
extlevel=1
```

MediaVision ProAudio and ProAudio Spectrum

[mvproaud.drv] (*the port is not specified here because there may be only one choice for this device, or because the I/O address is determined by the device driver when it loads or as it is read and assigned by the device driver in the CONFIG.SYS file*)
dma=1
irq=5

MediaVision Jazz and Jazz16

[jazz.drv] (*as above, the I/O address is self-determined or assigned in the CONFIG.SYS file*)
dma=1
irq=5

Number 8: Windows SETUP Indicates Not Enough Memory to Run SETUP

This message reflects less of a "conflict" than a configuration dilemma, but it can become a common aggravation in the process of cleaning up your system configuration or performing upgrades. This message may be presented during a number of possible upgrade and configuration activities, among them:

❖ using the Windows **SETUP** program to add or change video cards, driver files, or display resolutions

❖ using the Windows **SETUP** program to add or change network features

❖ using the Fonts feature under the Windows Control Panel to add display and printer fonts

❖ reinstalling Windows

There are two common causes and related cures for the problem:

Possibility A: The WIN.INI File Is Too Large

The most common cause for the appearance of this error message is that your **WIN.INI** or **SYSTEM.INI** file for Windows configuration exceeds 32,768 bytes in size. These files often increase in size if you have installed a lot of printer or screen fonts, or application programs that add a lot of parameter lines to these files. The **WIN.INI** file contains more information and thus grows faster and larger than the **SYSTEM.INI** file. If Windows finds the critical elements that it needs to load and run in the first 32,768 bytes or characters of the **WIN.INI** file, you can prevent the above error message.

A quick fix is to rearrange the contents of the **WIN.INI** file. This is done with a text editor (DOS **EDIT** or Windows' **NOTEPAD** programs) to move some elements within the file to a different place in the file. You should be familiar with the Cut and Paste features of the editor of your choice.

Below are a listing of the groups of information in the **WIN.INI** file. (These are not the actual files, as they do not contain the full details that are to be found in the files.) By rearranging the sections of **WIN.INI,** at least by moving the [sounds] section to the bottom of the file, you can move the file's critical setup sections within the first 32,768 characters. The [fonts] section should be near the top of the file, because fonts are critical to the appearance of Windows. Since the Windows **SETUP** program is used to change video configurations and these video configuration changes often affect the [fonts] section, **SETUP** needs to be able to find it in the file.

NOTE

When you rearrange the groups of information in the following listings, move the detailed information that follows each bracketed group heading (in the actual file, but not shown here) with the heading; the heading will be the first line of the entire group.

Primary Windows Environment Details at the Top

```
[windows]
[Desktop]
[intl]
[MS User Info]
[colors]
[ports]
```

Screen and Printer Appearance Items

```
[FontSubstitutes]
[TrueType]
[fonts]
```

Printer Specifics Below

```
[PrinterPorts]
[devices]
[Canon BJ-200ex,LPT1]
```

```
[Epson FX-86e,LPT2]
[Generic/Text Only]
[PostScript,LPT1]
[PostScript,LPT3]
[PSCRIPT]
[HP LaserJet Series II,LPT1]
[spooler]
[Network]
[Extensions]
[mci extensions]
```

Windows-Applications–Specific Details

```
[Compatibility]
[embedding]
[Windows Help]
[Cardfile]
[drawdib]
```

Applications-Specific Details (these have been alphabetized for clarity)

```
[CorelGraphics4]
[GenigraphicsDriver]
[Genigraphics GraphicsLink]
[Microsoft Graph 3.0]
[Microsoft Query]
[Microsoft System Info]
[Microsoft Word 2.0]
[MSAPPS]
[MS Proofing Tools]
[MS Setup (ACME) Table Files]
[MS Shareres]
[MSWrite]
[Paintbrush]
[pcdos]
[Visual CD]
```

```
[WAOL]
[WinFax]
[WinComm]
[WinZip]
```

Text and Graphics Conversions (these usually are large sections)

```
[MSWord Text Converters]
[MS Graphic Import Filters]
[MS Spreadsheet Converters]
[MS Text Converters]
[MS Graphic Export Filters]
```

Sounds at the End

```
[sounds]
```

End of WIN.INI File

If your **WIN.INI** file is less than 32,768 bytes in size, the next possibility is probably the cause of **SETUP**'s error message.

Possibility B: There Are Too Many .INF Files in the WINDOWS\SYSTEM Directory

The second most common cause of the message saying there's not enough memory to run Windows SETUP comes from having too many **SETUPx.INF, OEMSETUP.INF,** or **OEMx.INF** files (where *x* represents numbers to differentiate many separate filenames) in your disk drive's **C:\WINDOWS\SYSTEM** subdirectory (assuming C: is the letter of your disk drive). These files are used by the Windows **SETUP** program to allow you to select from a variety of hardware options for video display adapters, sound cards, and so on. You may move the files that are named **OEMx.INF** to a spare or backup subdirectory, or delete them from your disk.

Number 9. Windowed DOS Applications Appear Fuzzy, or Colors Are Changed Between Windows and Windowed DOS Sessions

If you click on the MSDOS icon under Windows, it usually opens a full-screen DOS session within Windows (no frame, dialog boxes, Windows wallpaper, and so on); but you do you have the option of opening a window and running DOS applications in the window instead. This is controlled by a selection for each DOS application by its **.PIF** file.

Fuzzy windowed DOS applications and changing colors are caused by the Windows drivers for your video adapter, or how your video adapter uses portions of upper memory, and the possibility that your memory manager or Windows is using a portion of upper memory that the video driver needs to use. To solve the problem, one or two memory management changes are necessary.

The first possible solution is to add command-line modifiers to *exclude* the B000-B7FF or B000-BFFF upper memory range in the configuration of your memory manager in the **CONFIG.SYS** file. These ranges are used for placing DOS text on your video screen. Usually Windows and memory managers avoid this area because of this, but a Windows device driver for some video cards may conflict with the memory manager and cause display problems for DOS text applications running in Windows. Using the text editor of your choice, open the **CONFIG.SYS** file for editing, and if your EMM386 or QEMM command lines look like the first lines in the groups below, change them to appear as the lines that follow them:

For EMM386, change from:

```
DEVICE=C:\DOS\EMM386.EXE RAM
```

To:

```
DEVICE=C:\DOS\EMM386.EXE RAM X=B000-B7FF
```

Or:

```
DEVICE=C:\DOS\EMM386.EXE RAM X=B000-BFFF
```

For QEMM, change from:

```
DEVICE=C:\QEMM\QEMM386.SYS RAM ROM ST:M
```

To:

```
DEVICE=C:\QEMM\QEMM386.SYS RAM ROM ST:M X=B000-
B7FF
```

Or:

```
DEVICE=C:\QEMM\QEMM386.SYS RAM ROM ST:M X=B000-
BFFF
```

Save the **CONFIG.SYS** file and exit the editor. Then reboot your system for these changes to take effect. Then run Windows, open a DOS Window session, do what you did before to cause the problem to happen, and see if your problem has gone away.

If not, try the next step.

Recent versions of DOS and Windows include a file named **MONOUMB.386** or **MONOUMB2.386.** This is a special device driver file to be used within Windows to keep it from conflicting with the video memory range in the upper memory blocks (UMBs). Locate this file on your DOS diskettes or on your hard disk. If it is not in the **C:\WINDOWS\SYSTEM** subdirectory, copy it from where you find it to that subdirectory. If you find a file named **MONOUMB.38_** or **MONOUMB2.38_** instead, you will have to be at a DOS prompt and invoke the **EXPAND** program that comes with Windows to decompress the file. The command line to use for this is:

```
EXPAND MONOUMB.38_ MONOUMB.386[Enter]
```

or

```
EXPAND MONOUMB2.38_ MONOUMB2.386[Enter]
```

When this file is properly in place in your **C:\WINDOWS\SYSTEM** subdirectory, the **SYSTEM.INI** file in the **C:\WINDOWS** subdirectory needs this device added under the [386Enh] section, to appear as follows:

```
[386Enh]
device=monoumb.386
```

or

```
[386Enh]
device=monoumb2.386
```

Save and close the **SYSTEM.INI** file and restart Windows, repeating the steps that previously caused the display problem. If the problem has not gone away after both of these changes have been made, you should check with your system or video card vendor to obtain technical support or new video driver files. In the meantime, if you want to keep on working but with reduced resolution and colors, you can use the Windows **SETUP** program to reconfigure Windows to use a "plain-old" VGA video driver and avoid the special video drivers entirely until the problem can be fixed properly through contact with vendor technical support or the help of a more experienced user.

Number 10: But I Really Need to Use More than Two COM Ports at One Time...

Using two COM ports at the same time is fairly common, as many systems are configured with a serial port mouse on COM1: and a modem on COM2:, and these two ports do not have the same IRQ assignment. If the use of a third port is required, it would *logically* have to be COM3:, but this port would normally be assigned to use IRQ 4, which conflicts the COM1:.

NOTE The examples in this section may be used as guidelines for editing your **SYSTEM.INI** file if the options presented in Windows' Control Panel/Ports/Settings/Advanced... dialogs are not sufficient to define your special configuration circumstances. Each of the three examples provides command lines to be entered under the [386Enh] bracketed heading in **SYSTEM.INI**; there will be lots of other configuration lines starting at the [386Enh] brackets before getting to any "COM..." lines).

If you have a system with a Micro Channel or EISA data bus, you can simply add a third COM port and share IRQs between COM ports 1 and 3 or 2 and 4, which must be specified in the Windows **SYSTEM.INI** file by adding the following line under the [386Enh] section:, as indicated in Example A:

Example A:

```
COMIrqSharing =1
```

This option applies *only* to Micro Channel and EISA systems. For ISA or non-Micro Channel, non-EISA systems, this line must be left set to 0 (zero) or NO, or not be present.

For non–Micro Channel, non-EISA systems, one solution may be to find an unused IRQ line that can also be configured on the COM3: port. Unfortunately, most add-in COM ports were designed with the original PC design and configuration rules in mind and provide switches or jumpers for the conventional IRQ settings for COM ports—IRQ 3 or 4. If your add-in COM port board allows you to assign an IRQ other than 3 or 4 to one of your new COM ports, and one of those IRQs is not in use by another device, do so, and then use Windows' `Control Panel` to indicate the new IRQ for the COM port of interest. If you *can* assign a unique IRQ to each COM port, you need to tell Windows which IRQ goes with a specific port. (IRQs 5 and 7 are simply examples here.) Example B is representative of this new configuration.

Example B:

```
COM3Irq=7
COM4Irq=5
```

(Technical hint: An electronics technician may be able to make an electrical modification to the add-in card IRQ connections to allow you to select IRQs other than 3 or 4.)

The remaining option is to seek out and purchase one of many special COM port add-in cards that provide non-standard

COM port addressing (COM port addresses other than 3F8h, 2F8h, 3E8h, or 2E8h) and additional IRQ options. These cards are typically used by people who operate electronic bulletin board systems (BBSes) under Windows or other operating systems. Inquire of your local computer dealer, a local BBS, or one of the popular on-line service forums (CompuServe, America Online, etc.) for specific information in locating one of these boards.

If you put one of these special-purpose COM port options in your system, you may need to tell Windows exactly where these ports are addressed and which IRQ goes with a specific port. Addresses 130h and 138h and IRQs 5 and 7 in Example C aren't necessarily accurate for any particular card.

Example C:

```
COM3Base=0130
COM3Irq=7
COM4Base=0138
COM4Irq=5
```

Bonus Points

Though not conflict resolutions, two more sets of command lines will be helpful here.

The following four lines really help the performance of communications programs running under Windows. These lines would be added at the end of the [386Enh] section of your **SYSTEM.INI** file.

COMBoostTime=100 (*this line gives comm programs more of Windows' time for high- speed data transfer*)

COM2FIFO=1 (*include a line like this for all of the COM ports that have a 16550A UAR/T chip*)

COM2Buffer=12 (*this line augments the "FIFO" specifier for high-speed data transfer*)

COMIRQSharing=

Add the following lines to [NonWindowsApp], which is below the [386Enh] section:

CommandEnvSize=1560 (*should match the /E:#### setting in the* SHELL= *line of **CONFIG.SYS.**) ("####" indicates a numeric variable value*)

FontChangeEnable=1 (*allows you to scale fonts in a Windowed DOS dialog screen*)

MouseInDOSBox=1 (*requires that a DOS mouse driver is loaded before running Windows—which allows you to use a mouse for DOS programs running under Windows*)

Summary

With the background information about the design of PC systems, a set of rules and examples, and these quick hints, you should have eliminated the most common system conflicts and have a really "clean" and functional system configuration. Our final chapter will walk through examples of using some of the commonly available system-information and diagnostic software to determine the system configuration and confirm that it functions properly.

CHAPTER 6

Tools, Tricks, and Tips

Topics covered in this chapter:

- ❖ Environment Report
- ❖ Memory Map
- ❖ IRQ/DMA
- ❖ BIOS Configuration
- ❖ Disk Configuration
- ❖ PCI Configuration
- ❖ Managing the Configuration of Microsoft Windows
  - ❖ IniExpert
  - ❖ RemoveIt
- ❖ What's-In-That-Box
- ❖ Preparing Information for Technical Support

This chapter is about using system information tools for collecting and sorting out the myriad of technical details you or someone else may need to know about your system. These tools will help us fulfill the configuration management we discussed in Chapter 1. We'll discuss the software that shows what resources are in use in a typical system configuration. This is information that most software and hardware companies ask for when you call technical support. We'll also cover some other handy software tools that make dealing with your computing environment a lot more pleasant.

You may already know that your system is a 486-something, that it has a *bunch* of memory, a *big* hard drive, and a fax/modem, and that it connects to some kind of network in your office. You may even know what kind hard drive you have, what class of fax/modem is installed, and what type of network you're connected to. However, when you call for technical support and they start playing "20 Questions" about addresses,

IRQs, and such, you may not have any idea how to answer these questions. Using these tools, you'll have the answers.

What If You Don't Know What Your Configuration Is?

There are numerous software tools available that detect and report tremendous amounts of information about PC systems. Some of these tools simply report on the items found in lower memory, ports, video modes, disk drives, etc., without actually testing for the presence of these devices. Advanced software tools, the ones you really need to use, show details about generic ports and devices, including what their IRQ assignments should be and possibly are.

DISK

So far we've only found one software tool that is aware of a significant number of specific hardware items, by generic type and specific brand and model. This software can accurately identify I/O addresses and IRQ and DMA assignments, and this tool, DiagSoft's QAInfo program, is provided on the diskette included with this book.

As good as any software program may be—and many are very good and can save you a lot of work—there are some cases in which it is necessary to physically inspect the hardware itself, to determine specific jumper or switch settings. Table 6.1 lists the general types of information we can get, and the information we cannot get, from system information software. The Vendor-Specific Information column refers to additional information that may be provided or devices that may be supported if the software developer has designed the software to extract and report this additional information.

TABLE 6.1 CONFIGURATION INFORMATION YOU CAN AND CANNOT GET FROM SYSTEM INFORMATION SOFTWARE

Information Type	Generic Information	Vendor-Specific Information	Unavailable Information
System Manufacturer	None	Usually read from the BIOS (see " Limitations," below)	
Machine Type	PC, PC/XT, PCjr, PC/AT, (generic AT, includes 80286, 80386, 80486, and Pentium)		
System Board Data Bus Type	ISA, EISA, Local Bus, or PCI		
CPU Type	i8086, i8088, NEC v20, NEC v30, i80286, i80386sx, i80386dx, i80486sx, i80486dx, i80486dx2, i80486dx2, i80486slc, Pentium, most Cyrix 80286-80486 upgrade chips by model #		
CPU Manufacturer	Generic/Intel, NEC, Cyrix		AMD (see "Limitations," below)
NPU (math chip)	i8087, i80287, i80387	Weitek, other non-Intel	
Base Memory	0-640K		

continued...

continued...

Extended Memory	Amount of memory, up to 16M in AT-class systems Up to 64M by AT standard in 386, 486, and Pentium systems	Greater than 64M with specific manufacturers' support (see "Limitations," below)	
Expanded Memory	Amount of memory and the software device driver version		EMS board mfr.
Shadowing/ Cache	No generic info except CPU cache for Intel 486+ parts	Vendor-specific chip and system board chipset information can be but is not always supported	Special-case shadowing or cache functions where system mfr. no longer exists to support this
BIOS Information		internal info if present and read from BIOS chip	Any available
Keyboard	Keyboard type		
Video Card	Monochrome, CGA, EGA, VGA	Video card make, model, BIOS, video RAM, with vendor support or generic VESA VBE presence	Monitor size, type, mode, display content

continued...

continued...

Serial Ports	Logical device assignment; hardware address; IRQ	UAR/T chip type as 8250, 16450, 16550, and 16550A; SMC and National Semiconductor parts	Generic chip manufacturers
Parallel Ports	Logical device assignment; hardware address; IRQ	SMC or National Semiconductor parts; enhanced modes	Generic chip manufacturers
Diskette Drives	Presence and drive letter assignment for: 160K, 180K, 360K, 720K, 1.2M, 1.44M, 2.88M		Diskette size
Hard Drives	Presence, drive letter, and capacity	Physical and logical disk drive parameters; SCSI & IDE: drive geometry, firmware version, and mfr.	MFM/RLL drives: drive manufacturer
SCSI Devices	Presence only if assigned logical device (drive letter)	Host adapter mfr. info; Adaptec parts/interfaces; ASPI driver; attached device type; SCSI ID#; host adapter address, IRQ, DMA	
CD-ROM Drives	Presence only as DOS logical drive letter	Disk content type (all via **MSCDEX** driver program); specific device driver or drive ID support per vendor	

continued...

continued...

Pointing Device	Presence; 2- or 3- button type	Mfr. details only if specific driver and device supported	
Game Port	Port presence		Joystick or device type
Network		Specific vendor/ protocol support required for presence, IRQ, boot ROM, DMA, card make/model	
Sound Cards		Creative Labs, MediaVision, Sierra Semiconductor, Aria, Roland MIDI, Microsoft Sound System	

Limitations to Obtaining System Information

There are many cases where the original equipment manufacturer (OEM) or designer has provided for certain capabilities beyond the design standards for PC, XT, or AT systems. In order to detect and report on these capabilities, the system information software designer must obtain specific, detailed information about any and all systems and devices from each equipment designer. The software must then be enhanced to make use of this specific information. Getting this updated software into the hands of all users is a tremendous task, and it's not always as complete a process as we might like it to be. Yet being aware of these limitations is good information to have as you inspect your system configuration using these tools.

For the best results in detecting hardware information, you should boot your system without loading any device drivers or running any memory resident programs. This is called a "clean boot," which is easily accomplished with versions 6.0 and higher of DOS by pressing the **F5** key to bypass loading of your **CONFIG.SYS** and **AUTOEXEC.BAT** files when you see the `Starting MS-DOS` or `Loading PC-DOS` message on your screen when your systems starts up. If one or more devices in your system requires a device driver to become active and detectable, use the **F8** key when the startup message line appears, to begin selectively loading individual device drivers. (Consult your DOS documentation for details about these two startup features.)

Keeping Some Parts a Secret

Some information about a feature or component may be completely unavailable except by visual inspection of the components involved, due to proprietary designs, manufacturing license agreements, various legalities, or design limitations.

Some manufacturers want their devices to appear to be generic devices, or possibly even to look like someone else's device. This is the case for some microprocessors, and you may notice that even if you have a sound card in your system and it's not Creative Labs' Sound Blaster card, the system information you get tells you it's a Sound Blaster. This is because your sound card emulates or works just like a Sound Blaster.

No Two System Setup Programs Are the Same

Many users want a tool to help them edit or save the system setup information that's stored in CMOS RAM. This information, consisting primarily of date, time, video display type, amount of memory, hard drive types, and diskette drive information, is otherwise accessible only at the time of system startup or by a special setup program provided with the system. Unfortunately, beyond the AT-standard information originally designed by IBM, most systems now have highly customized setup information.

System designers have used the system setup to control and hold information about CPU caches, memory timing, daylight savings time, enhanced disk drives, I/O ports, or other features. This information is different from that of the AT-standard information and is not stored the same way in all systems. Since systems change so frequently, with new features added or some taken away, and there are different BIOS programmers all over the world, it is nearly impossible to provide an independent setup program for most of the systems that exist.

All the Memory That's Fit to Use, But Not Detect

Many new systems provide systems that hold and address memory up to 256M or higher. This requires customizations to the system BIOS and other design considerations, and identifying this much memory requires utility and information program designers to work closely with the system manufacturers to learn how to detect and test such tremendous amounts of RAM. The same is true for various external or "level 2" CPU caches and other memory controls that are not covered by existing design standards.

Device Driver Thwarts Detection

One of the most common causes for a piece of system information software to miss the identification of a piece of hardware or its IRQ or DMA usage is the existence of a device driver program. Device drivers are typically loaded and run on your system through the **CONFIG.SYS** file when the system starts up. While these drivers may be essential to the functionality of your system or a specific device for normal, workaday applications programs, they can hide or intercept the hardware details necessary for a proper identification.

If your choice of system information software misses detecting a device that you know is in your system and working properly, try using the software after starting your system without device drivers. (As mentioned earlier, in versions of DOS from 6.0 on, this "clean boot" can be accomplished by pressing the **F5** key when the screen indicates Starting MS-DOS... or Loading PC-DOS.... This will bypass the loading of device drivers at bootup.) Conversely, some devices require that a device driver is loaded at startup before the device becomes active and available for detection.

Similarly, if you run any of these programs under Windows or OS/2, the reported system information can change significantly because these environments place several device drivers and their own device control programs between the hardware and application programs. Be aware that since system information programs are designed to interface with the hardware directly for proper detection, the use of such programs and their results may be unpredictable or cause Windows or OS/2 to crash or lock up.

Keeping Up with the Joneses

As PC systems and add-in devices are developed and introduced to the market so rapidly, few if any software programmers can detect the new features and update their software fast enough so that identification of the most recent devices is always available in any program on store shelves or direct from the software producer. It's important to understand that if you have a piece of hardware that was just designed in June 1995, and you are using software that was updated even as recently as March

1995, there's a very good chance that the new hardware will not be identified by the "old" software. As magical as software is, it still hasn't been able to overcome the time-space continuum.

Software that can identify the new data buses and the devices connected to them is under constant development and will appear with time. It is likely that more software will also identify Plug-and-Play BIOS and PnP devices and their configuration separate from the system and applications software that uses them.

These limitations do not have a tremendous impact on our configuration work, because those items we have the most trouble with still use the original IRQ, DMA, and I/O address resources we have become familiar with, and detecting activity on or the use of these resources is fairly standard as PCs go. For finding and reporting these resources, we'll see how to use and explore system information software.

Gathering Hardware Configuration Information

In this section, we will show you the types and variety of information you can obtain about your PC system using system-information or hardware-configuration reporting software. With an understanding of the limitations of this type of software, and the limitations imposed through some hardware designs, as we discussed above, you may find yourself overwhelmed or underwhelmed with the information reported to you.

Our primary concerns are the system resources of IRQ, DMA, and I/O address assignments. In almost all of the system information programs available, at least the I/O address assignment of many common devices is not reported, simply because it has been taken for granted that a specific device always uses a specific address, and this configuration resource cannot be changed. If some of these fixed configuration items could be changed, our task of configuration management would become many times more difficult. Having some known, standard, unchanging devices makes our job easier in some ways, even though it may appear to limit other configuration options.

Using QAInfo

QAInfo contains the system-information–gathering part of DiagSoft's QAPlus/fe and QAPlus/Factory products used by technicians, power users, and PC system and device manufacturers. It is a very powerful tool that addresses your system hardware and devices directly and specifically to obtain detailed device identification information.

QAInfo will run under DOS, Windows, or OS/2. The information obtained when running the program under Windows or OS/2 may differ slightly from that obtained when running under DOS because Windows and OS/2 place several device drivers between the hardware and the software. In some cases under these environments, your system may freeze or crash when using QAInfo or similar system information utilities because of the device drivers or the memory protection used in the operating systems.

None of this unpredictable behavior is destructive, but it can be annoying. This behavior is usually caused by a poorly designed device that is installed in your system, one which mistakenly responds to program instructions for another device that the program is trying to detect. To control this behavior, QAInfo provides a program control file, **QAINFO.INI,** that can be modified, as we'll see following.

Installing and Running QAInfo

QAInfo is provided with one support file, **QAINFO.HLP,** on the diskette with this book, and this file is in ready-to-use form. To keep the program handy and easy to use, you may make a new subdirectory for it and copy the files from the diskette onto your hard drive.

First, create a new subdirectory for QAInfo on your disk drive (assuming it's drive C:). Key in:

```
md qainfo[Enter]
```

Then copy the QAInfo files from the diskette (assuming it's drive A:, but it may be drive B: for you) to this new subdirectory by keying in:

```
copy a:\qainfo.* c:\qainfo[Enter]
```

Then change to the new subdirectory:

```
cd \qainfo[Enter]
```

Then execute the main program file:

```
qainfo[Enter]
```

The first time you run the **QAINFO** program, it tells you that it is initializing and creates a third file, **QAINFO.INI**, which is used to configure the program's operation. The initial screen will look like this:

```
Initializing...
QAINFO.INI file created. Continue? (y/n)
```

At this point, keying in **y** and then pressing **Enter** will take you to the opening menu shown in Figure 6.1. Leaving the program is as simple as pressing the **Esc** key to back out of the report display screens, pressing **x** at the opening screen, or selecting the **Exit** choice from the main menu.

FIGURE 6.1. QAINFO OPENING SCREEN.

Each item above the **Exit** selection represents a separate information-gathering operation. The two most critical to our conflict and configuration concerns are the **Hardware Configuration** and **IRQ/DMA** selections, but we will briefly discuss each selection in the order it appears.

The **Save Data Files** selection allows you to save data files containing the information reported by each information-gathering selection. Normally, unless there is a solid diamond in this field indicating it's been selected, the information reported by each menu item is not saved on your disk. To select this option, press **S** or move the menu highlight bar to this selection and press **Enter**. The data files will contain plain ASCII text of the reported items that appear on each screen. These files may be printed out, saved for your system inventory records, or uploaded to a technical support department to save a lot of support time. These files are replaced by new information each time you select an information-gathering item from the menu. The files that will be saved are named for the information they will contain, as follows:

TABLE 6.2 QAInfo Report Data Files

Information Report	Filename
Hardware Configuration	**HARDWARE.DAT**
Device Drivers	**DEVDVR.DAT**
Environment	**ENVIRON.DAT**
Memory Map	**MEMMAP.DAT**
IRQ/DMA	**IRQDMA.DAT**
BIOS Configuration	**BIOS.DAT**
Disk Configuration	**DISK.DAT**
PCI Configuration	**PCICFG.DAT**

Controlling What QAInfo Detects

The **QAINFO.INI** file that QAInfo creates when it is first run contains several lines of text that control which devices are detected during hardware, IRQ, and DMA reporting. This control is provided so that you can selectively disable specific device detection in case your system locks up during use of the program. The contents of this file are as follows:

```
[hardware]
CPU Type=y
Machine Type=y
NPU Type=y
BASE Memory=y
```

```
EXT Memory=y
EXP Memory=y
Video Adapters=y
Logical Drives=y
BIOS HDDs=y
BIOS FDDs=y
Clock Type=y
COM Ports=y
LPT Ports=y
Mouse=y
EMM Driver=y
Game Ports=y
XMS Memory=y
Sound Board=y
MIDI Port=y
Bus Type=y
SCSI HA=y
Network=y
Special Adapters=y

[irq]
Standard=y
IPX=y
Mouse=y
Network=y
WDNetwork=y
3Com EtherLink II=y
On-board Mouse=y
InPort Mouse=y
Com port=y
Lpt port=y
Hard disk=y
Adaptec SCSI=y
WD SCSI=y
Video retrace=y
AIC6260/6360 SCSI=y
UltraStor 14F=y
```

```
Aria Sound=y
Sound Blaster=y
Roland MIDI=y
AdLib=y
ST-0x SCSI=y
TMC-1800 SCSI=y
TMC-950 SCSI=y
Spurious=y

[dma]
Standard=y
IPX=y
Network=y
3Com EtherLink II=y
Adaptec SCSI=y
AIC6260/6360 SCSI=y
UltraStor 14F=y
Aria Sound=y
Sound Blaster=y
```

Each item in the list represents a type of information or device that QAInfo can detect. Under the [hardware] section, the entries control detection of types of devices or information. Under the [irq] and [dma] sections, the entries control detection of these resources for very specific hardware devices. A y after an entry indicates that QAInfo will try to detect this type of information or device. Changing the y to an n will prevent detection of a specific device.

While QAInfo has undergone extensive and very detailed and careful development so that it behaves well with all known hardware and system configurations, there are always a few systems, configurations, or unusual pieces of hardware that do not conform to expected and standard hardware design and operations. If the process of gathering information about your system seems like it's getting into the realm of black magic when you have devices that are not identified, or that conflict with other devices such that you can't identify the ones you know exist, you may wish to consult with a PC technician or your system vendor for assistance.

Any unpredictable behaviors or unusual results that occur when you run programs like QAInfo usually happen when IRQ or DMA assignment detection is performed. This is because the program must actually control the specific device to get an interrupt or DMA "reaction" from it. If another device conflicts with the one you are trying to detect, erratic program behavior is possible. Such problems usually manifest themselves by causing the system to freeze or to reboot by itself.

To isolate the types of devices that may cause this behavior, you can edit the **QAINFO.INI** file using DOS **EDIT** or Windows **NOTEPAD** or a similar text-only editor, and change the selection of one or more devices. Experience shows that detection of IRQs for certain sound card types, network cards, or the Microsoft InPort mouse interface card seem to encounter the most conflicts. To eliminate these most common possible detection problems, you might edit the [irq] section of your **QAINFO.INI** file to look like the following:

```
[irq]
Standard=y
IPX=y
Mouse=y
Network=y
WDNetwork=y
3Com EtherLink II=y
On-board Mouse=y
InPort Mouse=n
Com port=y
Lpt port=y
```

```
Hard disk=y
Adaptec SCSI=y
WD SCSI=y
Video retrace=y
AIC6260/6360 SCSI=y
UltraStor 14F=y
Aria Sound=n
Sound Blaster=y
Roland MIDI=n
AdLib=n
ST-0x SCSI=y
TMC-1800 SCSI=y
TMC-950 SCSI=y
Spurious=y
```

Notice that in this example the entries for InPort Mouse, Aria Sound, Roland MIDI, and AdLib have been set to **n** so that the program does not try to perform IRQ detection on these devices.

If disabling IRQ detection for only these devices does not solve any problems during the IRQ detection phase, then disabling all of the IRQ detection items as well as disabling DMA detection for all items should be tried first. If problems still exist, it is possible there is a more significant hardware problem in your system that needs to be diagnosed.

If the problem goes away and QAInfo runs fine with all device detection turned off, re-edit the file to enable detection one device at a time until the problem reoccurs. Then leave that device disabled, and continue to enable subsequent devices one at a time. You may find that detection of one or more devices or a combination of devices causes the improper program behavior. This constitutes a trial-and-error situation that you may want to leave to someone more skilled, as the technical aspects involved as program behavior changes can be tedious and considerable. Because of the nearly endless combinations in which devices may be turned on and off, someone with more experience or intuition about PC hardware may arrive at a solution much faster. Similar concerns exist for any program that deals so closely and specifically with the hardware.

Hardware Configuration

The QAInfo hardware configuration report is one of our first lines of defense in system conflict battles. Without knowing the basic contents or inventory of devices installed in your system, no configuration can be made conflict-free except by luck or trial and error. Figures 6.2 and 6.3 illustrate a typical system hardware configuration report.

FIGURE 6.2. FIRST PAGE OF QAINFO HARDWARE CONFIGURATION REPORT.

```
DiagSoft QAInfo  v5.30                    Copyright (c) 1989-1995 DiagSoft, Inc.

    DOS Floppy Drives .... A:[1.44M] B:[1.2M]
    CDR Drives .......... G:
    Clock Type .......... AT
    COM Ports ........... COM1[3F8h] COM2[2F8h]
    LPT Ports ........... LPT1[378h]
    Mouse Driver ........ none
    Game Ports .......... none
    PCMCIA .............. none
    Plug and Play BIOS ... none
    Network Card ........ Netware IPX
    SCSI Host Adapter .... Adaptec 154x[0330h]




                          PgUp      PgDn      ESC
ESC exits     F1 Help
```

FIGURE 6.3. *SECOND PAGE OF QAINFO HARDWARE CONFIGURATION REPORT.*

Here's a line-by-line explanation of the report that appears in Figures 6.2 and 6.3:

Processor Type: The identity of the PC's microprocessor.

Numeric Processor: The identity of the PC's math processor.

Bus Type: A listing of the bus type(s) in your system.

Base Memory Size: The amount of memory configured for DOS use.

Ext Memory, Available: The total amount of extended memory, and how much of it is available. (An XMS manager such as **HIMEM.SYS** may consume all of this memory.)

XMS Driver Version: The version of the XMS device driver software.

XMS Memory: The total amount of extended memory managed by an XMS driver (such as **HIMEM.SYS**).

EMS Driver Version: The version of the LIMS-EMS device driver software.

EMS Memory, Available: The total amount of expanded memory, and how much of it is available.

Primary Video: Monochrome, Hercules, CGA, EGA, or VGA.

Video BIOS: The maker and version of the video adapter BIOS.

Text Base Address: The upper memory address that text information is sent to for display.

Video RAM Size: The amount of video RAM present on the video adapter.

Secondary Video: Monochrome, Hercules, CGA, EGA, or VGA.

Video Mode, EGA Switch: The current video display mode and status of the EGA register switches (a rather esoteric but available piece of information).

DOS Hard Drives: The size of hard drives available to DOS.

DOS Floppy Drives: The diskette drives available to DOS.

CDR Drives: The diskette drives available to DOS.

Clock Type: Whether a clock/calendar device exists, and its type, usually an AT type.

COM Ports: The logical COM ports and their physical addresses.

LPT Ports: The logical LPT ports and their physical addresses.

Mouse Driver: The version of the DOS mouse driver, if present.

Game Ports: The number of game (joystick) ports available.

PCMCIA: The number of slots and cards present, if any.

Plug-and-Play BIOS: If present, the version number.

Network Card: The protocol type and device address.

SCSI Host Adapter: The adapter type and address, or "ASPI" if managed by a SCSI device driver.

Sound Card: If present, will indicate Aria, MediaVision, Sound Blaster, or Microsoft Sound System.

Device Drivers

The device drivers report from QAInfo provides information that is technically interesting, and functional for programmers, but is perhaps too detailed for most users, unless this information is pertinent to technical support transactions when troubleshooting a software configuration or function. Figure 6.4 shows a typical Device Drivers report. The items reported are defined below.

```
DiagSoft QAInfo  v5.30                    Copyright (c) 1989-1995 DiagSoft, Inc.

    DOS Device Drivers:
    Address  |Name      |Attributes
    
    0103:0048 |NUL       |8004 char, nul
    05F3:1FDE |G:-L:     |48C2 drive, ioctl, removable, logical
    D297:0000 |NDOSSTAK  |C000 char, ioctl
    D1B5:0000 |CON       |C053 char, ioctl, logical, console, stdout, stdin
    CEA4:0000 |ASPICD0   |C000 char, ioctl, removable
    CCA8:0000 |SCSIMGR$  |C000 char, ioctl
    027C:0000 |EMMXXXX0  |C000 char, ioctl
    0248:0000 |XMSXXXX0  |A000 char, printer
    0070:0023 |CON       |8013 char, console, stdout, stdin
    0070:0035 |AUX       |8000 char
    1A8E:195E |PRN       |8800 char, removable
    0070:0059 |CLOCK$    |8008 char, clock
    0070:006B |A:-F:     |48C2 drive, ioctl, removable, logical
    0070:007B |COM1      |8000 char
    1A8E:1970 |LPT1      |8800 char, removable
    1A8E:1982 |LPT2      |8800 char, removable

                         PgUp      PgDn      ESC
ESC exits     F1 Help
```

FIGURE 6.4 QAINFO DOS DEVICE DRIVERS REPORT.

Address: The actual memory address that the device driver has been loaded into and occupies as it runs.

Name: The internal process, device, or program name of the device driver.

`Attributes`: What type the device driver is (by internal numeric designation, whether it handles data one character at a time (`char`), handles data in blocks, or is a disk drive), and what other devices or specifics pertain to the particular type of device. For instance, the second item listed applies to disk drive devices that respond to internal (BIOS and DOS) features known to programmers as "ioctl" functions, some of them may be removable, and they have logical designations. The fourth entry, `CON`, is a character device that responds to ioctl functions; it is logical, it is the system console (keyboard and monitor), and it responds to or provides data by the internal `stdin` and `stdout` functions.

Environment Report

This report is simply a display of all of the DOS environment variables, where they are located in memory, and how much memory space they take up (see Figure 6.5).

```
DiagSoft QAInfo  v5.30              Copyright (c) 1989-1995 DiagSoft, Inc.

 DOS Environment:
 Address 0580:0000, Length 1568, Used 415

 CONFIG=DOS_FULL
 COMSPEC=C:\DOS\COMMAND.COM
 BPATH=:e:\brief\macros
 BHELP=e:\brief\help
 BFLAGS=-i120k7Mrt -mJWA -D101key
 COM-AND=D:\CA
 DIRCMD=/a
 MIDI=SYNTH:1 MAP:E
 NU=C:\N
 PGPPATH=D:\PGP
 TEMP=C:\TEMP
 TMP=C:\TEMP
 TZ=PDT
 WINS=C:\WINDOWS
 WINDOWS=C:\WINDOWS
 WINDOWSS=C:\WINDOWS

                    PgUp     PgDn     ESC
 ESC exits    F1 Help
```

FIGURE 6.5 *QAInfo DOS Environment Report.*

`Address`: Indicates the actual memory location where the DOS environment variables are stored.

Length: Indicates the total allocated size of the memory reserved for DOS environment variables. This value may be specified on the SHELL= line of your **CONFIG.SYS** file.

Used: Indicates the total allocated size of the memory used by the DOS environment variables that DOS or you have set.

The remaining list of items represents the DOS environment settings, as you might see them by using the DOS SET command at a DOS prompt.

Memory Map

The memory map report from QAInfo tells us what programs or functions are loaded into the system's memory, which location and how much memory a program is using, what type the program is, and which software vectors are controlled by the program. (See Figure 6.6.) This listing, and the device driver listing, can tell you or someone in a technical support role if specific device drivers or programs are loaded and available for use. This can be important if, for example, you have trouble with a sound card and need to determine if the device driver for that card is active in system memory.

```
DiagSoft QAInfo  v5.30                    Copyright (c) 1989-1995 DiagSoft, Inc.

  DOS Memory Map by Segment Address:
   Addr │ Size │ Owner    │ Type          │ Hooked vectors
  (0247)│ 10576│ *SYSTEM  │ data          │
  (0248)│   816│ HIMEM    │ device driver │
  (027C)│  2368│ EMM386   │ device driver │ 30 67
  (0311)│  5552│ FILES=   │ DOS parameter │
  (046D)│    80│ FCBs=    │ DOS parameter │
  (0473)│   512│ BUFFERS= │ DOS parameter │
  (0494)│  1152│ LASTDRV= │ DOS parameter │
  (04DD)│    64│ *SYSTEM  │ program       │
  (04E2)│    48│ *DOS_A   │ data          │
  (04E6)│  2368│ *DOS_A   │ program       │ 22 24 2E
  (057B)│    64│ *FREE    │ free          │
  (0580)│  1568│ *DOS_A   │ environment   │
  (05E3)│ 11136│ SMARTDRV │ program       │ 15 19
  (089C)│   160│ *FREE    │ free          │
  (08A7)│ 40224│ LSL      │ program       │ E5 E7 E9 EC F5
  (127A)│ 13744│ NE2100   │ program       │ 72 EB

                       PgUp      PgDn      ESC
 ESC exits    F1 Help
```

Figure 6.6 *QAInfo System Memory Map Report.*

Address: The starting address location where the program is stored and runs in memory.

Size: The amount of memory the program occupies.

Owner: The name (internal to the program, BIOS, or DOS) that the program loads by, not the DOS filename.

Type: Whether the program is a device driver, part of the program's own unique data area, an item stored as part of the DOS environment, or a DOS parameter, or if this entry represents the actual presence of the program itself in memory, as well as if the memory area is free or unused.

Hooked Vectors: The software interrupt vectors that are controlled by a specific program or device driver. Software interrupt vectors are internal program control points available through the BIOS or DOS that can be accessed by other programs. They provide access to various internal software services and functions. They are not related to the hardware interrupt signals.

IRQ/DMA

Two of the most important hardware resources in your system configuration are reported in the IRQ/DMA menu selection in QAInfo. This report also contains a listing of your BIOS and DOS versions. Two screens full of information are shown to give you an illustration of these resources.

As you may find yourself exploring various different system information programs, you might notice one distinct difference from most programs. This difference is in the reporting of DMA channel assignments. DiagSoft's products are the only ones that do a thorough and accurate job of reporting DMA channel use for known, supported devices.

```
DiagSoft QAInfo  v5.30                Copyright (c) 1989-1995 DiagSoft, Inc.

  IRQ/DMA detection

  System Software:
      ROM BIOS: Award
      BIOS Date: 09/26/94
  DOS Version: 7.00

  DMA Channel Usage:
  DMA 0: Available *
  DMA 1: Available *
  DMA 2: Floppy
  DMA 3: IPX
  DMA 4: [CASCADE]
  DMA 5: Adaptec 154x
  DMA 6: Available *
  DMA 7: Available *

  Interrupt Assignments:
  IRQ 00: Timer
                            PgUp     PgDn     ESC
ESC exits     F1 Help
```

FIGURE 6.7 *FIRST PAGE OF THE QAINFO IRQ/DMA REPORT.*

All eight DMA channels are listed in this report, indicating which device uses a specific channel, or that a channel is possibly available. In the sample report in Figure 6.7, only three DMA channels are in use—2, 3, and 5—and one is shown as [CASCADE] or otherwise unavailable because this channel is used to link the second of two DMA controllers to the first. You might also expect to see one or two functions of your sound card using separate DMA channels.

```
DiagSoft QAInfo  v5.30                Copyright (c) 1989-1995 DiagSoft, Inc.

  IRQ 00: Timer
  IRQ 01: Keyboard
  IRQ 02: [CASCADE]
  IRQ 03: COM2(2F0h)
  IRQ 04: COM1(3F8h)
  IRQ 05: Available *
  IRQ 06: Floppy
  IRQ 07: Available *
  IRQ 08: Clock/Cal
  IRQ 09: OCCUPIED
  IRQ 10: IPX
  IRQ 11: Adaptec 154x(330h)
  IRQ 12: Available *
  IRQ 13: NPU
  IRQ 14: OCCUPIED
  IRQ 15: Available *
  no IRQ: LPT1(378h)

  * Not used by any standard device
                            PgUp     PgDn     ESC
ESC exits     F1 Help
```

FIGURE 6.8. *SECOND PAGE OF THE QAINFO IRQ/DMA REPORT.*

Hardware IRQ lines are listed in numeric order, and the identity of the device that is using that IRQ line follows. The program will attempt IRQ and DMA detection for any device that's found in the hardware configuration and that's supposed to generate IRQ or DMA signals. In this configuration, there are no shared or conflicting IRQs. Device LPT1: exists at address 378h but is listed as not having an IRQ assignment, by the "no IRQ:" label. The program determined by checking the hardware configuration that an LPT1: device is installed in the system, but in checking for an IRQ assignment for this device, one was not detected. Technically speaking, no IRQ activity could be detected coming from LPT1: in this case, because it is necessary for a program to actually cause signal activity on a parallel port before it can be detected.

If you have more than one device using an IRQ or a DMA channel, all of those devices will be reported on the line following the IRQ or DMA number. The report does not specifically indicate conflicts as being conflicts because the presence of multiple devices on one IRQ or DMA channel line may not be in conflict if the devices are not active at the same time. The text and examples in previous chapters should be used to help you evaluate potential conflict conditions.

To generate known signal activity that can be detected, QAInfo requires that a special test connector be attached to the actual parallel port socket on the PC to properly and accurately create and detect IRQ activity on parallel ports. It is possible that an attached printer could generate an error signal, such as running out of paper, coincident with this program looking for IRQ activity on the parallel port, but that is not predictable or likely. Programs that claim to indicate or detect IRQ activity on parallel ports *without* a special test connector for signal readback are suspect as to their accuracy.

**OTHER
REFERENCE**

To build your own test connector, specific for use with DiagSoft's QAPlus-family of products, see Appendix F for details.

Those IRQs listed as Available * did not have any interrupt activity from any known, standard, or specially supported devices. Except in the case of the LPT port, which we would expect to generate an IRQ signal on IRQ 7 because it is designed to have this IRQ assignment, it is reasonable to assume that the IRQs so marked are indeed available for use in your configuration.

Another listing is possible, that of Spurious:, which indicates that an IRQ signal was generated from some unknown source at a time when no activity was expected. Such cases are rare, but they should cause you to suspect technical problems inside your system. In this case, it is recommended that you obtain a diagnostic program to check your system thoroughly for hardware defects.

BIOS Configuration

The BIOS information report isn't too exciting, but it does help to confirm some of the information shown in the hardware configuration report. The information in this report is extracted from the BIOS data area of lower memory. It shows what the BIOS, and likely DOS, have assigned for some of the common devices, specifically the physical addresses for the logical devices assigned as COM and LPT ports.

This information is determined by the BIOS at system startup. The information given in the hardware configuration report is obtained by individual detection of the actual devices, much like the BIOS does it. Any discrepancy between this report and the hardware configuration report is cause to suspect a problem with the system BIOS, the system board, or an add-in device, or the presence of a device driver that may be altering the BIOS information after startup.

```
DiagSoft QAInfo  v5.30                    Copyright (c) 1989-1995 DiagSoft, Inc.

    BIOS System Information

    BIOS Type:

        Copyright:     Award     Date: 09/26/94

    Video Information
        Display Mode:    03h
        Columns:         80
        Buffer Length:   4096 bytes
        Start Offset:    0000h
        Cursor Type:     00h
        Active Page:     0

    ROM BIOS I/O Data
        COM1 Address:    03F8h    Timeout = 1
        COM2 Address:    02F8h    Timeout = 1
        LPT1 Address:    0378h    Timeout = 20
        LPT2 Address:    03BCh    Timeout = 20
                            PgUp     PgDn     ESC
ESC exits    F1 Help
```

FIGURE 6.9 QAINFO BIOS INFORMATION REPORT.

```
DiagSoft QAInfo  v5.30                    Copyright (c) 1989-1995 DiagSoft, Inc.

        Buffer Length:   4096 bytes
        Start Offset:    0000h
        Cursor Type:     00h
        Active Page:     0

    ROM BIOS I/O Data
        COM1 Address:    03F8h    Timeout = 1
        COM2 Address:    02F8h    Timeout = 1
        LPT1 Address:    0378h    Timeout = 20
        LPT2 Address:    03BCh    Timeout = 20
        LPT3 Address:    03BCh    Timeout = 20

    Disk Information
        Floppy Status:      00h
        FDC Status:         C0h
        Fixed Disk Status:  03h
        HDC Status:         00h
        Fixed Disk Count:   01
        Error Status:       0000h
                            PgUp     PgDn     ESC
ESC exits    F1 Help
```

FIGURE 6.10 QAINFO BIOS INFORMATION REPORT, SECOND PAGE.

This report shows devices and their parameters as BIOS has detected them at system startup. The items listed, except for the I/O addresses for the COM and LPT ports listed under ROM BIOS I/O Data, are of little significance to our configuration concerns, but they may be of interest to some programmers or technical support personnel. The ROM BIOS I/O Data address information for logical devices and their physical addresses should compare identically with the information listed in the hardware configuration report and the IRQ/DMA listings. If the logical devices and physical addresses do not compare, it is possible that a device driver or some other program is altering the data detected by the BIOS, or is interfering with QAInfo's device detection. (See "Limitations to Obtaining System Information," near the beginning of this chapter.)

Disk Configuration

This report gives us details about the physical and logical disk drive partitions that are in the system. This information is generally valuable for you to have available, but it does not play a significant role in the context of the hardware configurations we are addressing.

Figure 6.11 is an example from a system using a large SCSI hard drive, where the SCSI host adapter provides a special translation of the drive's Cyl/Hd/Sec information, rather than the actual parameters for this particular hard drive. Translation is a feature provided by some disk drive adapters to all large disk drives to be compatible with DOS. (The issues of disk drive, partitions, and translations are not within the context of this book. Details may be found in the documentation for your PC system, disk drive adapter, disk drive, or DOS.) The second screen is from a system using an IDE disk drive, which indicates a more typical disk drive description without special translation values.

```
DiagSoft QAInfo  v5.30                    Copyright (c) 1989-1995 DiagSoft, Inc.

    Disc Partitions
    Fixed Disc # 1
      Partition # 1
      Type:  (bootable)

      Starting Cyl/Hd/Sec:  0/1/1
      Ending Cyl/Hd/Sec:  63/62/63
      Boot Sector Info
        ID String:  'IBM  7.0'
        Bytes per Sector:      512      Media Byte:               F8h
        Sectors per Track:      63      Sectors per Cluster:       16
        Heads per Cylinder:    255      Total Sectors:        1028097
        Sectors per FAT:       251      Number of FATs:             2
        Boot Sectors:            1      Root Dir Entries:         512

      Volume Size:     502.0MB
    Partition # 2

      Starting Cyl/Hd/Sec:  64/0/1

                              PgUp       PgDn      ESC
ESC exits     F1 Help
```

FIGURE 6.11 QAINFO DISK CONFIGURATION
REPORT: LARGE SCSI DRIVE

```
DiagSoft QAInfo  v5.30                    Copyright (c) 1989-1995 DiagSoft, Inc.

    Disc Partitions
    Fixed Disc # 1
      Partition # 1
      Type:  (bootable)

      Starting Cyl/Hd/Sec:  0/1/1
      Ending Cyl/Hd/Sec:  521/31/63
      Boot Sector Info
        ID String:  'MSWIN4.0'
        Bytes per Sector:      512      Media Byte:               F8h
        Sectors per Track:      63      Sectors per Cluster:       32
        Heads per Cylinder:     32      Total Sectors:        1052289
        Sectors per FAT:       129      Number of FATs:             2
        Boot Sectors:            1      Root Dir Entries:         512

      Volume Size:     513.0MB
    Fixed Disc # 2
      Partition # 1

                              PgUp       PgDn      ESC
ESC exits     F1 Help
```

FIGURE 6.12 QAINFO DISK CONFIGURATION REPORT: IDE DRIVE

PCI Configuration

This report lists specific details about the presence of a PCI bus
in your system, as well as any and all PCI devices installed in
the system and detected by this part of the QAInfo program.

```
DiagSoft QAInfo  v5.30                    Copyright (c) 1989-1995 DiagSoft, Inc.

  PCI Information
  PCI Bus #0
  Slot #0
     Vendor - 'INTEL CORP.'
     Device - '82430 Chipset'
     Device class is Bridge of type Host
  Slot #1
     Vendor - 'ADAPTEC'
     Device ID is 5078h
     Device class is Mass Storage controller of type SCSI
  Slot #2
     Vendor - 'INTEL CORP.'
     Device - '82375EB PCI-EISA'
     Class ID is 00.00.00
  Slot #3
     Vendor - 'DIGITAL EQUIPMENT COMPANY'
     Device ID is 0002h
     Device class is Network Controller of type Ethernet
  Slot #4

                        PgUp      PgDn      ESC
ESC exits    F1 Help
```

FIGURE 6.13 *QAINFO PCI INFORMATION REPORT*

PCI Bus #: A heading for the devices connected to individual PCI bus controllers.

Slot #: A heading for each item connected to a PCI bus controller. Because PCI devices may be built onto the system board, these items may in fact not occupy an add-in card slot connection.

Vendor: The manufacturer of the device identified by or addressed as a PCI bus slot.

Device: The device occupying the slot.

Device class: Either a numerical or a text description of the device in a slot. A numerical description is more technical and represents specialized components connected as PCI bus devices. There are many common device classes: a "bridge" representing the actual PCI bus interface to the CPU, "mass storage" representing disk drives, "network controller" representing network interface components, and so on. In Figure 6.13, an EISA I/O bus controller acts as a component on the PCI bus.

Managing the Configuration of Microsoft Windows

There are at least two major hassles when dealing with Windows: managing its configuration, and adding or removing installed programs. The two tools we'll be looking at in this section provide a tremendous amount of support for you and your Windows configurations.

As you may know, simply deleting a group or program icon from Windows does not remove that program or all the files it added to your system. After upgrading or changing to a new program, or trying to delete an old one, you don't always know which files the program installed onto your system or what changes were made to your **WIN.INI** and **SYSTEM.INI** files. Removing an old program can be tedious work, and may leave behind several megabytes of unused files. The RemoveIt utility from Vertisoft helps you manage this situation.

As you work with Windows, learn about its quirks, and find ways to configure it, you have probably encountered a lot of references to the configuration items contained within several different Windows configuration files. Without collecting a shelf full of various Windows "expert" books, you could find yourself making all sorts of alterations to these files and not be certain of the expected results. Several utility packages are available to help with the process of identifying and sorting out the dozens of Windows configuration commands, but one stands out as simple, fast, and clean—IniExpert from Chattahoochee Software.

The following two sections are only brief highlights of these two featured tools, as we don't intend to cover the vast realm of Windows configurations, but these highlights should give you some incentive to consider these tools for your own use. After all, once you have your system hardware configuration perfected, it may be time to do something about the on-screen environment you work with.

IniExpert

I'm not sure how anyone configuring Windows lived without this program. Rather than flipping through hundreds of pages of various books and manuals dealing with the configuration details of Windows, use this one simple utility program to get access to all of the standard, documented features of the Windows **WIN.INI, SYSTEM.INI, PROGMAN.INI, CONTROL.INI,** and **WINFILE.INI** files. This program lets you browse and edit these files. It also comes with a feature called IniSave, which backs up your **WIN.INI** and **SYSTEM.INI** files every time you run Windows. This utility is much more versatile and helpful than using the Windows **NOTEPAD** or **SYSEDIT** programs to access these files.

The sample screen in Figure 6.14 shows the selection of which Windows configuration file you want to edit indicated by the File Name: field; the section of this file to be edited, indicated by the Section: field; the entries in each section at the Entry: list; the Keyname or specific Windows parameter of interest within the chosen Section: entry; and the Value: field, where you can edit the keyname's value. The display area below the Value field provides helpful information about the selected entry.

The tool buttons to the right of the screen allow you to apply any changes to the configuration file, which will not take effect until you exit and restart Windows. If you don't want to make a change, simply exit IniExpert without saving the changes and go about your work. If you want help editing the various Windows configuration files on your system, IniExpert is a great tool. It will not replace becoming more familiar with

Windows through the program's documentation or other books, but it makes the work a lot easier. If you are completely unfamiliar with the Windows configuration files, it's best that you not alter them, with or without IniExpert's help.

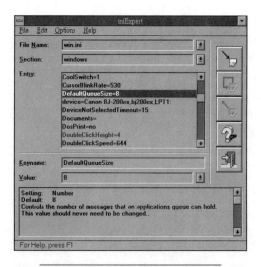

FIGURE 6.14 INIEXPERT MAIN SCREEN.

If you want to protect your Windows configuration through various upgrade and program installation phases, or simply learn about your configuration, this is a terrific tool to add to your collection.

RemoveIt

There are a lot of "uninstall" utilities around for Windows. These utilities keep track of all the files, Windows program groups, and subdirectories that are placed on your system when a new application is installed. If you later decide to remove a particular program, the uninstall utility remembers everything that was installed and can delete it from your system. This process prevents a lot of disk drive clutter left by program files that are no longer needed.

Ideally such a utility should be installed and used immediately after you have done a fresh Windows installation, and before installing all of your applications, so that you have an installation log of everything on your system. If you've decided to use one of these utilities on an existing and fully loaded Windows installation, some of these programs can still survey your disk drives to locate the bits and pieces of installed applications.

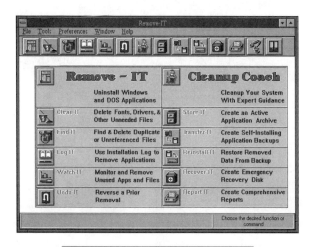

FIGURE 6.15 *REMOVEIT'S MAIN SCREEN.*

RemoveIt provides the basics of what an uninstall utility can do and adds a lot of additional features, including keeping track of whether or not certain device drivers and font files are used, so that if you want, you can remove files that are historically never used. Why waste precious disk drive space? The benefits do not stop here. If you would rather not completely uninstall a seldom-used application, you can have RemoveIt instead do an archived removal of an application by compressing and backing up all of an application's files so they're available for later reuse, but saving some disk space in the meantime.

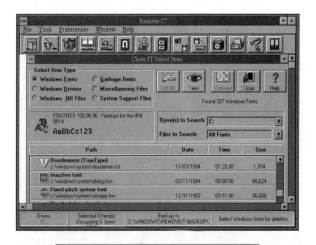

FIGURE 6.16 *REMOVEIT'S CLEANIT SCREEN.*

Perhaps the most interesting aspect of Version 2 of RemoveIt is its Upgrade Assistant feature, which can help you with an eventual installation of Windows 95. If you're like some of us, when you get Windows 95 you may not want to replace your existing Windows environment, preferring instead to install Windows 95 separately without affecting the currently installed version of Windows, so you can test drive Windows 95 before you decide to convert to it completely. Microsoft does not offer a way to simply add Windows 95 to your system and copy the program groups and icons you had. Installing Windows 95 always replaces your existing DOS bootup files, offering to back up your old DOS files in case you want to remove Windows 95 from your system and put the old DOS back in place. (The Windows 95 operating environment will not run under any prior version of DOS.) You can choose to either replace your existing Windows installation or install Windows 95 separate from the older version of Windows.

In the latter case, Windows 95 will not install your existing Windows program groups and applications in its configuration. To use your already-installed Windows applications under a separate installation of Windows 95, you have to install or select each existing application separately—which is a *very* tedious and time-consuming task.

Another way to accomplish this "test drive" is to completely duplicate your existing Windows configuration into another subdirectory (**\WIN95** works for me) and then install Windows 95 over this copy of Windows. This approach consumes a *lot* of disk drive space, as you end up with even more leftover, excess files which may never be used again. I don't know anyone who has *that* much disk space to waste.

RemoveIt's Upgrade Assistant feature does all of this tedious work for you, in a lot less time, using a lot less disk space (see Figure 6.17). Upgrade Assistant will inventory your current Windows configuration and indicate various parts of your present configuration that can be changed, as well as indicate any excess files that can be deleted to make room for Windows 95 to fit onto your disk drive. Upgrade Assistant will also present a variety of options for preserving your existing DOS and Windows files in the event you decide to go back to your original configuration as if you had never installed Windows 95 at all.

When this survey of the existing installation is complete, you are ready to install Windows 95. The survey process works even if you have already done a separate Windows 95 installation. The crucial aspect is to get a log of how Windows alone is configured. Once Windows 95 is installed and running, you invoke the Upgrade Assistant from within Windows 95 and begin to migrate your previous configuration to the newly installed environment. This migration is done in detail, including placing proper entries in Windows 95's system registry, which is used instead of most of the **WIN.INI** and **SYSTEM.INI** entries we've become accustomed to.

Once you have learned to use Windows 95 and have decided to stick with it, the Upgrade Assistant can be used again to remove your old DOS and Windows files, completing the upgrade and migration process.

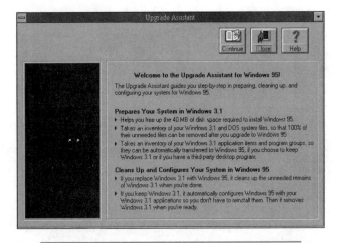

FIGURE 6.17 REMOVEIT'S UPGRADE ASSISTANT SCREEN.

What's-In-That-Box

We've included What's-In-That-Box, version III, on our diskette. It's a do-it-yourself tutorial about the layout, contents, and functions of the various devices inside your PC system.

The program is stored on the diskette in a compressed but self-extracting file format. The program can be run in DOS or under Windows, but it must be copied to your hard disk and prepared from a DOS prompt. To begin to use this program, first create a new subdirectory on your disk drive (assuming it's drive C:). Key in:

```
md whatsin[Enter]
```

Then copy the **WBOX3.EXE** file from the diskette (assuming it's drive A:, but it may be drive B: for you) to this new subdirectory by keying in:

```
copy a:\wbox3.exe c:\whatsin[Enter]
```

Then change to the new subdirectory:

```
cd \whatsin[Enter]
```

You can then delete the distribution file from your hard disk, because we're done with it, by keying in:

```
del wbox3.exe[Enter]
```

Then execute the main startup file:

```
begin[Enter]
```

From here, enjoy the show and learning more about your PC. We've left the screen shots out of this section to encourage your own discovery!

Preparing Information for Technical Support

Calling, e-mailing, or faxing for technical support may be something we have come to dread in our experience with PC hardware and software. It takes a lot of patience to wait through phone queues and time zones. The quest for technical support also requires a considerable amount of information exchange. Indeed, the lack of information—because of lack of experience, awareness, or the proper tools—creates a technical support bottleneck at all stages of the process. If you are paying for technical support from a pay-per-call service or a service contract, getting the best service for your money is critical. Books such as this one, and well chosen software tools, can take a lot of pressure off of everyone along the way.

We expect technical support people to be familiar with almost every aspect of PCs—from hardware to software. Indeed, this is not very practical or even possible, given the thousands of systems and programs that are in use. Those people who have become quite experienced and accomplished at providing technical support in one way or another are often elevated to design and development or management positions. The better someone is at technical support, the less time they spend doing it. It's to be hoped, though, that they will still be able to share and promote greater expertise among others. Some of us even begin to write books to share what we know.

Technical support people—and perhaps, all too often, system and program developers—expect users to be more familiar with their PCs and software. Obviously this is not always the case, and it may never be. Users should simply be able to use their systems and programs, through good design, planning, and training on these items, and not have to be able to design, build, or program them. (But if you try it, you might find it enjoyable and worthwhile!)

The burden of technical support, getting it and giving it, can be significantly relieved if all parties involved are adequately prepared and cooperative. The technical support person should be able to define the types of information needed to help resolve a problem. PCs are complex systems; a lot of aspects of them interact, and yes, conflict at times. Sorting all this out, if you haven't been able to do it with the help of this book, takes you another level deeper into the system details. You can be prepared for this, which will save time, and help you determine if you're getting the right help.

The information provided by the tools we've highlighted in this chapter, and the configuration details we've discussed throughout the book, are essential for effective technical support—yes, even the support of software. Keeping your system inventory current and having a report of your hardware, DOS, and Windows configuration information will save you several minutes of time in the technical support process. Being able to fax or file-transfer this information to the support department may be even more effective. You'll find this type of transaction becoming more and more popular as technical support shifts to on-line electronic means.

In addition to all of this technical information, you should be able to reproduce the conditions under which a problem occurs, and be able to communicate this effectively as well. If your problem is that your printer "doesn't print," the support process takes longer than it has to. You'll be encouraged to check the basics: Is the printer plugged in? Turned on? Connected to your computer? Is your software configured properly? A little system information and running a diagnostic program such as QAPlus can help reduce the possibilities of where the problem could be and get you on the right track to a solution much faster.

Certainly the more you know about your PC, the more you'll be able to get from the services you request to support it. Your knowledge will help you determine if you're a satisfied customer or need to seek out another service to help you. Since you picked up this book, you're obviously interested in becoming more familiar with your PC, either to support yourself directly or to determine if you're getting the right support. When you know more, share the information with others, and you'll begin to find that users helping other users creates a strong support network.

Summary

In closing our configuration management processes with this chapter, it's safe to say that we've covered a lot of ground in a short time. We've reviewed a lot of material which has taken many years for many people to accumulate, study, understand, and apply in daily practice, or through handy and essential software tools. We've seen how software and hardware can complement each other, and even how different types of software can be combined to make our PC configuration management quite complete, up to and including preparations for and transitions to new hardware and operating systems.

As with everything else in this fast-paced PC market, you can expect new systems and software revisions that may supersede some of the examples shown in this book. We'll try to keep pace with these developments, and will consider any and all input to the configuration process for future revisions to this work—perhaps even to some of the featured software tools. The PC business thrives on user ideas and needs. No idea, no conflict or problem goes unheard if you make it known.

Keep in touch, and *happy bits!*

Appendix A

System Configuration Detail List

Update the following list, or keep a printed or file copy of the system information reported by a utility program such as SYSCHK, QAPlus, Manifest, Norton's SysInfo, or MSD. This information is critical to any technical support needed.

Record the IRQ, DMA, and I/O address assignments as well as the make, model, version, and type for each device in your system.

Configuration Item	Item Details
System BIOS:	
CPU:	
Math Chip:	
CPU Speed:	
Bus Type:	
Total RAM:	
External Cache Size:	
Diskette Drives:	
Hard Drive Adapter Type:	
Hard Drive #1:	
Hard Drive #2:	
SCSI Devices:	
Disk Compression:	
Video Adapter:	
Video BIOS Version:	
Operating System:	
User Interfaces:	
COM1:	
COM2:	
COM3:	
COM4:	
LPT1:	
LPT2:	
LPT3:	
Mouse Type:	
Sound Card:	
Network Adapter:	
Modem:	
Other:	

Also keep a backup file or printed copy of the following files:

- ❖ **AUTOEXEC.BAT**
- ❖ **CONFIG.SYS**
- ❖ **WIN.INI**
- ❖ **SYSTEM.INI**

APPENDIX B

Standards and Participating Organizations

The following listing represents a majority of the official industry standards organizations that affect the PC industry. If you are a hardware designer or software programmer and need specific technical information about a technical specification or standard, these are the places to look. The information available from these organizations is exceptionally detailed and theoretical, and not generally useful for end-user tasks with PCs. These organizations do not maintain information about finished goods or vendor products.

If you are looking for less technical information, consult the bibliography references listed in Appendix C. If you are looking for vendor-specific information, you will find that most vendors provide direct end-user support on CompuServe, America Online, and the Internet, or are listed in many catalogs and magazines.

Organization	Type of Organization or Information	Electronic Information Resources
ANSI *American National Standards Institute* 1430 Broadway New York, NY 10018 (212) 354-3300 (212) 398-0023 (fax)	Computer, electronic, and other U.S. standards	
ATA *AT-Attachment Committee/Small Form Factor Committee*	IDE disk drive specifications	Subscribe to ATA mailing list through: majordomo@dt.wdc.com
CCITT *International Telecommunications Union* Place de Nations Ch-1211 Geneva 20, Switzerland 41-22-99-51-11 41-22-33-72-56 (fax) *Information Gatekeepers, Inc.* 214 Harvard Ave. Boston, MA 02134 (617) 232-3111 (617) 734-8562 (fax)	Modem and telephony specifications	
DMTF *Desktop Management Task Force* JF2-51 2111 N.E. 25th St. Hillsboro, OR 97124 (503) 696-9300	DMTF/DMI workstation and network management specifications	ftp.intel.com (look in /pub/IAL) www.intel.com

EIA

Electronics Industry
Association
Global Engineering
Documents
2805 McGaw Ave.
Irvine, CA 92714
(714) 261-1455
(714) 261-7892 (fax)
(800) 854-7179
(order info)

Computer and
electronics standards

EPA

Energy Star Computers
Program
(MC:6202J)
Washington, DC 20460
(202) 233-9114
(202) 233-9578 (fax)

Energy Star
compliance

IEEE

Institute of Electrical and
Electronic Engineers
The Standards
Department
445 Hoes Lane
P.O. Box 1331
Piscataway, NJ 08855-1311
(201) 562-3800
(201) 562-1571 (fax)

Computer and
electronics standards

Intel Corp.

5200 N.E. Elam Young
Parkway
Hillsboro, OR
97124-6497
(503) 696-2000

PCI, Plug-and-Play,
Advanced Power
Management specs

ftp.intel.com
www.intel.com

Microsoft Corp.

1 Microsoft Way	Plug-and-Play,	ftp.microsoft.com
Redmond, WA 98052	PC95, Advanced	www.microsoft.com
(206) 882-8080	Power Management	
	specs	

PCI

(Peripheral Component	System bus, built-in	ftp.intel.com
Interconnect)	and add-in card	www.intel.com
PCI Special Interest	specifications	
Group		
M/S HF3-15A		
5200 N.E. Elam		
Young Parkway		
Hillsboro, OR		
97124-6497		
(503) 696-2000		

PCMCIA

Personal Computer	Portable and desktop	BBS: (408) 720-9386
Memory Card Industry	system add-in devices	BBS: (408) 720-9388
Association		Internet news:
1030 East Duane Ave.,		alt.periphs.pcmcia
Suite G		CompuServe: GO
Sunnyvale, CA 94086		PCVENF, Lib 12
(408) 720-0107		
(408) 720-9416 (fax)		

Plug-and-Play

PLUGPLAY	Plug-and-Play	CompuServe: GO
	specifications	PlugPlay

SCSI

Small Computer	SCSI, SCSI-2, and	Subscribe to SCSI
Systems Interface	SCSI-3 specs	mailing list through:
		scsiadm@witchitaks.ncr.com

**Underwriters
Laboratory
Standards**

Underwriters Labs Inc.	Electrical and
1655 Scott Blvd.	safety testing
Santa Clara, CA 95131	
(408) 985-2400	

VESA

Video Electronics	Video BIOS
Standards Association	Enhancements
2150 North First St.,	(VBE), Local Bus
Suite 440	
San Jose, CA 95131-2029	
(408) 435-0333	
(408) 435-8225 (fax)	

APPENDIX C

Reference Materials

You will find the following books most helpful in your pursuit of the operational and functional aspects of PC systems, including repair and upgrade techniques.

Title	Author(s)	Publisher
Troubleshooting Your PC	Jim Aspinwall, Rory Burke, Mike Todd	MIS:Press
Inside the IBM PC	Peter Norton	Brady
Upgrading and Repairing PCs	Scott Mueller	Que
System BIOS for IBM PCs, Compatibles, and EISA Computers	Phoenix Technologies Ltd.	Addison-Wesley
Technical Reference, Personal Computer XT and Portable Personal Computer and *Technical Reference, Personal Computer AT*	IBM Corporation	IBM Corporation
DOS Programmer's Reference	Terry R. Dettman	Que

The technical reference manuals from IBM may be out of print, but available from a technical library or a friend.

NOTE

APPENDIX D

Favorite Software Tools, Assistance, Memory Management, and Access to Cyberspace

If you want to explore the world inside your PC or get more out of it, from the front end to a virtual world without borders, the programs listed below are highly recommended and well worth having. Frankly, We like to brag about other people's products, especially the ones that help with PC use so much, and that might also make us look like we really have a handle on this PC stuff. The commercial programs, listed first, are available in most software stores, or by phone or mail order from many sources. The Shareware programs are available from many bulletin boards and on-line services.

QAPlus, QAPlus/FE, and QAPlus/Win (DiagSoft)

QAPlus isn't just for technicians anymore! Every user can gain something valuable from having a good, solid PC diagnostic program on hand. At the very least, you can provide your own assurance that your system is working correctly—a must for before, during, and after upgrade and fix-it processes. Add to that the wealth of complete and accurate system hardware information, and you've started to become your own PC guru.

QAPlus/WIN is an excellent tool for checking out all of your system features under Windows, and it contains the unequaled RAM tests that make all of the QAPlus products so terrific. If that's not enough, QAPlus/WIN comes with built-in access to the Electronic Technical Support Center (ETSC). If one of QAPlus/WIN's tests detects a problem with your system, or if you simply have a question about hardware, DOS, or Windows, you can activate the ETSC features, compose your question or problem report, and send it off to the ETSC resources at DiagSoft. After a review of the problem or question, an answer is made available for you to download and apply to your system later. If technical support for the rest of the PC products and systems we have was this easy to obtain, there probably wouldn't be any more PC problems to deal with.

Look for QAPlus/2 (for OS/2) and QAPlus/95 (for Windows 95), due out soon! If you need a solid diagnostic tool for your Macintosh, look into Peace of Mind, also from DiagSoft.

Norton Utilities (Norton/Symantec)

If you're not already familiar with or using the popular Norton Utilities, We'd venture to guess that you've not had your system long enough to encounter a file or disk error more serious that DOS's **CHKDSK** or **SCANDISK** could fix. That's actually good news—disk drives and system components are getting more reliable. But they aren't perfect yet. For all of the times we've intentionally tried to break the file structure on my disk drives, We couldn't find a problem short of actually erasing a few critical disk sectors at a low level that Norton's Disk Doctor (NDD) and/or DISKFIX programs couldn't fix. The UNERASE program is quick and easy to use. Not only are there must-have utilities for your disk and file system, but the other file utilities provide services to a DOS-based system that should have been a part of DOS since the beginning. Most of the utilities also run under Windows.

IniExpert (Chattahoochee Software)

What Norton does for your disks and files, and tries to do for your Windows configuration, IniExpert excels at helping you keep track of and optimizing those confusing **INI** files that Windows depends so heavily on. This program takes you step-by-step through each and every standard Windows parameter in your **WIN.INI, SYSTEM.INI,** and **PROGMAN.INI** file, allowing you to make changes and explaining the significance of each parameter so you can understand what you are doing. IniExpert also keeps track of changes to your **INI** files and lets you restore the last known set of good working files in case a recent change produced less than desired results.

QEMM, SideBar, and Internet Suite (Quarterdeck Office Systems)

Quarterdeck gets a triple-billing here because we simply can't imagine using a PC without the tools and features they provide for regular use. Before many of us got "dragged" into the world of Microsoft Windows, many of us were users of DESQview, Quarterdeck's multitasking environment for DOS. DESQview led us to use QEMM as our memory manager, because no other memory manager of substance existed, and QEMM provides benefits with RAM that were unthinkable a few years ago. QEMM is simply faster, "smarter," and easier to use (and then take for granted) than anything like it you might imagine. It's always been reliable, and the company has always been responsive to users and technology. If you need to get the most out of your system's memory, you need QEMM. With QEMM you also get MANIFEST, an excellent system information tool worth its weight as a standalone utility.

Having been thrust into the world of Windows, it took years before someone provided a Windows desktop interface that was worthwhile, and like the benefits of QEMM, Quarterdeck has not let us down in bringing us SideBar, the company's replacement for the tired, clunky—okay, *ugly*—old interface of Windows Program Manager. Sidebar cleans up your PC's screen when you're using Windows, providing a new desktop environment that gives you the responsiveness you need to run programs and find your applications and files fast, and actually makes Windows a pleasure to use. Why add more clutter, slowdowns, and confusing controls with other Windows desktop managers when you can have near-perfection?

The Internet Suite is not the last of Quarterdeck's fine products, and not least, but it's our latest favorite since we've got our systems configured and finely tuned, have the memory managed, and have a user interface we can live with. Internet Suite is a soon-to-be-classic example of how we can enjoy the Internet, from surfing the World Wide Web to peeking at dozens of "ftp" sites for the latest files to keeping up with our on-line pen pals. Why bother with three or four different applications for handling your time on the Internet when one set of matched programs will more than satisfy your craving for life in cyberspace?

SYSCHK (Paul Griffith [Shareware])

Paul's program is a masterpiece of usability and simplicity for end users. SYSCHK provides the most complete and fun-to-use system information tool we've run across. Try it!! SYSCHK is available on CompuServe and from Paul's BBS at (408) 945-0242.

COM-AND (R. Scott McGinnis [Shareware])

COM-AND stands for "Communications And..." The "And" is almost unlimited. If you need to venture into raw on-line interaction, or want to try your hand at some powerful yet easy-to-grasp communications scripting, COM-AND should be your entry point. Scott has created an entire range of scripts and accessories for us to enjoy on-line communications, and he documents it all extremely well. Scott's program set is available on CompuServe and via the Support ETC BBS at (310) 439-7714. (On CompuServe, use the PC File Finder, GO PCFF, and search for the keyword COM-AND.) Dialing the BBS alone is a testimony to the power of the scripting language in COM-AND, because the BBS software has been created entirely with COM-AND scripts.

APPENDIX E

On the Disk

Some acknowledgments for and background about the programs provided on our diskette are warranted:

QAInfo (DiagSoft)

QAInfo is the most complete source of information about PC system IRQ and DMA assignments. It covers more hardware better than any other piece of independently developed software in the market. Only hardware manufacturers may know more about their devices, and some of them go to DiagSoft rather than try to create this kind of software themselves. Not only is QAInfo a standalone product used for system configuration evaluations, its main component is also part of DiagSoft's diagnostic products.

Some very skilled, clever, imaginative, and just plain excellent people at DiagSoft conceive and create these products, and continue their development on a regular basis to meet the demands of an ever-changing PC industry. No one else has met or exceeded that claim to date. Thank you, DiagSoft.

What's-In-That-Box (Jeff Napier)

Jeff has created *the* PC system tutor on a disk. Many others have tried to put this kind of visualization about what goes on inside a PC into writing, and we're not sure that any others have even scratched the surface compared to what Jeff has put into this program. Jeff's program is available on CompuServe. (Use the PC File Finder, GO PCFF, and search for the specified filename by Filename.) Please, if you like it, let him know about it by phone or CompuServe e-mail! (Contact information is provided in the **READ.ME** text file with the program.) Install this program on your hard disk and find out what all those gadgets are under your system's hood. Thanks, Jeff!!

Appendix F

QAInfo Parallel Port Loopback Plug

In order to accurately detect IRQ activity on parallel ports, QAInfo requires that a specially wired test connector be attached to all parallel (LPT) ports of interest.

This connector is very simple to make from commonly available parts: a male DB-25 data plug and five short pieces of wire. Many computer stores and electronics stores such as Radio Shack carry these plugs in do-it-yourself form with small crimp-on pins that may be inserted into the connector body. More-technical users will probably be able to dig into their "junk box" and come up with the necessary parts in a few minutes.

If you have more than one parallel port in your system, make one loopback plug, wired as shown below, for each port so you have to run the IRQ/DMA test in QAInfo only once to detect the IRQs and any conflicts. The connections indicated are made among the pins on the test connector, which is then plugged into the PC's parallel port socket.

The wiring of the test connector should be as follows:

- ❖ Pin 1 connects to Pin 13
- ❖ Pin 2 connects to Pin 15
- ❖ Pin 10 connects to Pin 16
- ❖ Pin 11 connects to Pin 17
- ❖ Pin 12 connects to Pin 14

GLOSSARY

8086

An Intel 8-bit external, 16-bit internal data bus microprocessor capable of addressing up to one megabyte of memory and operating at speeds up to 10MHz. Its companion numerical coprocessor or math chip is the 8087. The 8086 is found in the IBM PS/2 Models 25 and 30 and some clones.

8088

An Intel 8-bit internal, 8-bit external data bus microprocessor capable of addressing up to one megabyte of memory and operating at speeds up to 10MHz. This chip is used in the IBM PC, XT and compatible clone systems. Its companion numerical coprocessor or math chip is the 8087.

80286

An Intel 16-bit internal and external data bus microprocessor capable of addressing up to 16 megabytes of

memory and operating at speeds up to 12 MHz. Some non-Intel equivalents may run at 16MHz. This chip's first use in PC systems was in the IBM PC/AT. Its companion numerical coprocessor or math chip is the 80287.

80386DX

An Intel 32-bit internal and external data bus microprocessor capable of addressing up to 4 gigabytes of memory and operating at speeds up to 33 MHz. Some non-Intel equivalents may run at 40MHz. This chip's first use in PC/AT-compatible systems was by COMPAQ. Its companion numerical coprocessor or math chip is the 80287 in some systems, otherwise the 80387.

80386SX

An Intel 32-bit internal and 16-bit external data bus microprocessor capable of addressing up to 32 megabytes of memory and operating at speeds up to 25 MHz. Its companion numerical coprocessor or math chip is the 80387SX.

80486DX

An Intel 32-bit internal and external data bus microprocessor capable of operating at speeds up to 50 MHz. This processor contains an internal math coprocessor (floating point processor) and an 8kByte internal instruction cache.

80486DX2

An Intel 32-bit internal and external data bus microprocessor capable of operating at speeds up to 66 MHz internally due to a doubling of the external clock speed. This processor contains an internal math coprocessor (floating point processor) and an 8kByte internal instruction cache.

80486DX4

An Intel 32-bit internal and external data bus microprocessor capable of operating at speeds up to 100 MHz internally due to a quadrupling of the external clock speed. This processor contains an internal math coprocessor (floating point processor) and an 8kByte internal instruction cache.

80486SX

An Intel 32-bit internal and external data bus microprocessor capable of operating at speeds up to 25 MHz. It is equivalent to the 80486DX but doesn't provide the internal floating point processor or the 8kByte cache.

80486SX2

An Intel 32-bit internal and external data bus microprocessor capable of operating at speeds up to 50 MHz internally due to doubling of the external clock speed. It is equivalent to the 80486DX but doesn't provide the internal floating point processor or the 8kByte cache.

Adapter

A hardware device, usually a set of connectors and a cable, used between two pieces of equipment to convert one type of plug or socket to another, or convert one type of signal to another. Examples are a 9- to 25-pin serial port adapter cable, a serial port to serial port null modem, and a PC printer interface to printer cable.

Adapter Card

A plug-in card used to exchange signals between the computer and internal or external equipment. *See also* Parallel Adapter, Serial Adapter, Video Adapter, Disk Controller.

Add-in Card

See Adapter Card.

Address

A location in memory or on a hardware bus, of either a specific piece of data or a physical hardware device.

ANSI

American National Standards Institute. A governing body managing specifications for the computer industry and other disciplines. In terms of computing, ANSI maintains a set of standards for the coding and displaying of computer information, including certain "ESCape sequences" for screen color and cursor positioning. A device driver file, ANSI.SYS, can be loaded in your PCs CONFIG.SYS file so that your screen can respond properly to color and character changes provided from programs or terminal sessions between computers.

Application

A computer program, or set of programs, designed to perform a specific type or set of tasks, in order to make a computer help you to do your work or provide entertainment. Typical applications are games, word processing, database or spreadsheet programs.

AT

A model series of the IBM PC family known as Advanced Technology. This series includes those systems that use the 80286 microprocessor chip. The 'AT' classification has been applied to 80386 and 80486 based systems that offer basic compatibility with and enhancements over the original specification.

ATA

AT-Attachments. An industry wide specification for the interfacing of devices, typically hard disk drives, to the PC/AT standard data bus.

AT-compatible

A description of a personal computer system that provides the minimum functions and features of the original IBM PC/AT system, and is capable of running the same software and using the same hardware devices.

AUTOEXEC.BAT file

An ASCII text file that may contain one or more lines of DOS commands that you want executed every time you boot-up your PC.

Also known as just the 'autoexec' file, this file is customizable, using a text editor program, so that you can specify a DOS prompt, set a drive and directory path to be searched when you call up programs, or load terminate-and-stay resident programs that you want to have available all of the time.

Base address

The initial or starting address of a device or memory location.

Base memory

See DOS Memory.

BATch file

An ASCII text file that may contain one or more lines of DOS commands that you want to execute by calling for one file, the name of the batch file, rather than keying them in individually. Also known as just a 'bat' file, these files are customizable, using a text editor program, so that you can specify a DOS prompt, set a drive and directory path to be searched when you call up programs, or load and execute specific programs. Batch files are used extensively as short cuts for routine or repetitive tasks, or those that you just don't want to have to remember each step for. These files always have the extension '.BAT', as required by DOS.

BBS

Bulletin Board Service or Bulletin Board System. A public or private, local or remote computer system accessed by modem for message and/or file sharing between users. A BBS may be operated by anyone with the time, equipment and software to do so. User groups, clubs, companies and government agencies operate BBSes to share information. There may or may not be a charge for the use of some systems. Listings of BBSes may be found accompanying some communications programs, in the back of PC journals or in many phone book yellow pages. *See also* Online services.

BIOS

Basic Input/Output System. The first set of program code to run when a PC system is booted up. The BIOS defines specific addresses and devices and provides software interface services for programs to use the equipment in a PC system. The PC system BIOS resides in a ROM chip on the system board. BIOSes also exist on add-in cards to provide addition adapter and interface services between hardware and software.

Bootup

The process of loading and running the hardware initialization program to allow access to hardware resources by applications.

Bus

An internal wiring configuration between the CPU and various interface circuits carrying address, data and timing information required by one or more internal, built-in, add-in or external adapters and devices.

Byte

The common unit of measure of memory, information, file size or storage capacity. A byte consists of 8 bits of information. There are two bytes to a word (16-bits) of information. 1000 bytes is referred to as a kilobyte or kByte, and contains 1024 bits of information.

CGA

Color Graphics Adapter. The first IBM-PC color display system,

providing low-resolution (320x200) color graphics and basic text functions.

CMOS clock

A special clock chip that runs continuously, either from the PC system power supply or a small battery, providing date and time information.

CMOS RAM

A special memory chip used to store system configuration information. Rarely found in PC or XT models and usually found in 286 or higher models.

CMOS setup

The process of selecting and storing configuration (device, memory, date and time) information about your system for use during boot-up. This process may be done through your PC's BIOS program or an external (disk-based) utility program.

Command line

The screen area immediately after a prompt, where you are to key-in commands to the computer or program. This is most commonly the DOS command line, as indicated by the DOS prompt (C>, C:\> or similar).

CONFIG.SYS

An ASCII text file that may contain one or more lines of special DOS commands that you want executed every time you boot-up your PC. Also known as the 'config' file, this file is customizable using a text editor program, so that you can specify one or more items specific to how your system should operate when it boots up. You may specify device drivers (with DEVICE=) such as memory management programs, disk caching, RAM disks; the number of FILES and BUFFERS you want DOS to use; the location, name and any special parameters for your command processor (usually COMMAND.COM), among other parameters. Refer to your DOS manual or device driver software manual for specific information.

Controller

See adapter.

Conventional memory

Also known as DOS memory, this is the range of your PCs memory from 0-640 kilobytes, where device drivers, DOS parameters, the DOS

command processor (COMMAND.COM), your applications programs and data are stored when you use your computer. *See* Extended, Expanded, Video, High and Upper Memory.

CPU

Central Processing Unit. The main integrated circuit chip, processor circuit or board in a computer system. For IBM PC-compatible systems the CPU may be either an Intel or comparable 8088, 8086, 80286, 80386 (sx or dx), 80486 (sx or dx) or NEC V20 or V30 chip.

Current directory

This is the subdirectory you or a program has last selected to operate from, and that is searched first before the DOS PATH is searched when calling a program. *See also* Current disk drive and Logged drive.

Current disk drive

The drive that you have selected for DOS and programs to use before searching the specified drives and directories in the DOS PATH (if any is specified). This may also be the drive indicated by your DOS prompt (typically C> or C:\> or similar) or that you have selected by specifying a drive letter followed by a colon and the <Enter> key, as in A:<Enter>. This is also known as the 'logged' drive.

DESQview(tm)

A multitasking user-interface that allows simultaneous operation of many programs. DESQview uses Expanded Memory to create virtual-DOS sessions and memory areas, and controls the amount of processor time given to each DOS session and the application using it.

DESQview/X(tm)

A multitasking graphical user-interface based on the MIT X-Window client/server standard. It allows simultaneous operation of many programs, on the local system and across other X-Window-based systems on a network. DESQview/X uses Expanded Memory to create virtual-DOS sessions and memory areas, and controls the amount of processor time given to each DOS session and the application using it.

Device

An actual piece of hardware interfaced to the computer to provide input or accept output. Typical devices are printers, modems, mice, keyboards, displays, and disk drives.

There are also some special or virtual devices, handled in software that act like hardware. The most common of these is called NUL, which is essentially 'nowhere'. You can send screen or other output to the NUL device so that it does not appear. The NUL device is commonly used if the actual device to send something to does not exist, but a program requires that output be sent someplace. NUL is a valid 'place' to send output to, although the output really doesn't go anywhere.

Device driver

A special piece of software required by some hardware or software configurations to interface your computer to a hardware device. Common device drivers are ANSI.SYS used for display screen control, RAMDRIVE.SYS which creates and maintains a portion of memory that acts like a disk drive, and HIMEM.SYS, a special device driver used to manage a specific area of Extended memory, called the HMA. Device drivers are usually intended to be used in the CONFIG.SYS file, preceded by a DEVICE= statement.

Diagnostics

Software programs to test the functions of system components.

Directory

File space on disks used to store information about files organized and referred to through a directory name. Each disk has at least one directory, called the Root directory, which is a specific area reserved for other file and directory entries. A hard disk Root directory may contain up to 512 other files or directory references, limited by the amount of disk space reserved for to Root directory entries. The files and directories referred to by the Root directory may be of any size up to the limit of available disk space. Directories may be thought of as folders or boxes, as they may appear with some graphical user-interfaces, though they are not visually represented that way by DOS. *See* Root Directory and Subdirectories. All directories, except for the Root directory, must have a name. The name for a directory follows the 1-8 character restrictions that apply to filenames. *See also* Filename.

Disk

A rotating magnetic medium used for storing computer files. *See also* Diskette and Hard Disk.

Diskette

Also called a floppy diskette, this is a disk media contained in a cover

jacket that can be removed from a disk drive. The term floppy is synonymous with flexible, in that the disk medium is a magnetically coated disk of thin plastic material.

Disk drive adapter or controller

A built-in or add-in card interface that provides necessary connections between the computer system I/O circuits and a disk drive.

DMA

Direct Memory Access. A method of transferring information between a computer's memory and another device, such as a disk drive, without requiring CPU intervention.

DOS Diskette

A diskette formatted for use with DOS-based PCs and file system.

DOS memory

Temporary memory used for storage of DOS boot and operating system information, programs and data during the operation of your computer system. DOS memory occupies up to the first 640k of RAM (Random Access Memory) space provided in your system's hardware. This memory empties out or loses its contents when your computer is shut off.

DOS or Disk operating system

A set of software written for a specific type of computer system, disk, file and application types to provide control over disk storage services and other input and output functions required by application programs and system maintenance. All computers using disk drives have some form of disk operating system containing applicable programs and services. For IBM-PC-compatible computers the term 'DOS' is commonly accepted to mean the computer software services specific to 'PC' systems.

DOS System Diskette

A diskette formatted for use with DOS-based PCs and file system, that also contains the two DOS-system hidden files and COMMAND.COM to allow booting up your system from a diskette drive.

Drive

The mechanical and electronic assembly that holds disk storage media, and provides the reading and writing functions for data storage and retrieval.

EGA

Enhanced Graphics Adapter. A color graphics system designed by IBM, providing medium-resolution text and graphics, compatible also with monochrome text and CGA displays.

EISA

Extended Industry Standard Architecture. The definition of a PC internal bus structure that maintains compatibility with IBM's original PC, XT and AT bus designs (known as the ISA, Industry Standard Architecture) but offering considerably more features and speed between the computer system and adapter cards, including a definition for 32-bit PC systems that do not follow IBM's MCA (MicroChannel Architecture).

EMM

Expanded Memory Manager. The term often given to the software, or that refers to Expanded memory chips and cards. *See also* Expanded Memory.

EMS

Expanded Memory Specification. The IBM-PC-industry standards for software and hardware that makes up Expanded memory.

ENTER (<Enter>)

The command or line termination key, also known as 'return' on your keyboard. There are usually two <Enter> keys on your keyboard. Under some applications programs these two keys may have different functions; the numeric keypad <Enter> key may be used as an "enter data" key while the alphanumeric keyboard <Enter> key may be used as a Carriage Return.

Environment

An area of memory setup used by the DOS software to store and retrieve a small amount of information that can be shared or referred to by many programs. Among other information that the DOS environment area could hold are the PATH, current drive, PROMPT, COMSPEC, and any SET variables.

ESDI

Enhanced Small Device Interface. A standards definition for the interconnection of newer high-speed disk drives. This standard is an alternative to earlier MFM, coincident applications of SCSI, and recent IDE drive interfaces.

Execute

The action that a computer takes when it is instructed to run a program. A running program is said to execute or be executing when it is being used.

Executable File

A program file that may be invoked from the operating system. DLLs and overlay files also contain executable program information, but their functions must be invoked from within another program.

Expanded Memory

This is an additional area of memory created and managed by a device driver program using the Lotus-Intel-Microsoft Expanded Memory Specification, known also as LIMS-EMS. There are three common forms of EMS; that conforming to the LIMS-EMS 3.2 standard for software-only access to this memory, LIMS-EMS 4.0 in software, and LIMS-EMS 4.0 in hardware. With the proper hardware, this memory may exist and be used on all PC systems, from PCs to 486 systems. Expanded Memory may be made up of Extended Memory (memory above 1 megabyte) on 386 and 486 systems, or it may be simulated in

Extended Memory on 286 systems. LIMS-EMS 3.2, 4.0 (software) and 4.0 (hardware) are commonly used for additional data storage for spreadsheets and databases. Only LIMS-EMS conforming to the 4.0 standard for hardware may be used for multitasking. Expanded memory resides at an upper memory address, occupying one 64k block between 640k and 1 megabyte. The actual amount of memory available depends on your hardware and the amount of memory you can assign to be Expanded Memory. The 64k block taken up by Expanded Memory is only a window or port giving access to the actual amount of EMS available. There may be as little as 64k or as much as 32 megabytes of Expanded Memory.

Extended Memory

This is memory in the address range above 1 megabyte, available only on 80286 or higher systems. It is commonly used for RAM disks, disk caching, and some applications programs. Using a special driver called HIMEM.SYS, or similar services provided with memory management software, the first 64k of Extended Memory may be assigned as a High Memory Area which some programs and DOS can be loaded into.

File

An area of disk space containing a program or data as a single unit, referred to by the DOS file directory. Its beginning location is recorded in the file directory, with reference to all space occupied by the file recorded in the DOS File Allocation Table(FAT). Files are pieces of data or software that you work with on your computer. They may be copied, moved, erased or modified, all of which is tracked by DOS for the directory and FAT.

Filename

The string of characters assigned to a disk file to identify it. A filename must be at least one, and may be up to 8 leading characters as the proper name. A filename may be followed by a 3 character extension, separated from the proper name by a period(.). Allowable filename and extension characters are: A-Z, 0-9, !,@,#,$,^,&,_,-,{,},(,).',`,or ~. Also, many of the IBM Extended character set may be used. Reserved characters that cannot be used are: %, *, +, =, ;, :,[,], <, >, ?, /, \, |, " and <Space>. Filenames must be unique for each file in a directory, but the same name may exist in separate directories. Filenames are assigned to all programs and data files.

Filename extension

A string of 1-3 characters used after a filename and a separating period (.), with the same character limitations as the filename. The extension is often used to identify certain types of files to certain applications. DOS uses BAT, EXE, and COM as files it can load and execute, thought this does not preclude the use of these extensions for non-executable files. The extensions SYS, DRV, and DVR are commonly used for device driver programs that are loaded and used in the CONFIG.SYS file prior to loading DOS (as COMMAND.COM.) Refer to your software documentation for any limitations or preferences it has for filename extensions.

Fixed disk

See Hard disk.

Floppy disk

See Diskette.

Gigabyte (Gbyte or GB)

A unit of measure referring to 1,024 megabytes or 1,073,741,824 bytes of information, storage space or memory. Devices with this capacity are usually large disk drives and tape backup units with 1.2 to 2.8 Gigabytes of storage area.

Hard disk

A sealed disk drive unit with platters mounted inside on a fixed spindle assembly. The actual platter is a hard aluminum or glass surface coated with magnetic storage media. This definition also suits removable hard disks in which the hard platters are encased in a sealed casing, and mate with a spindle similar to the attachment of a floppy diskette to the drive motor. The platters are sealed to keep foreign particles from interfering with and potentially damaging the platters or the read/write heads that normally maintain a small gap between them during operation.

Hardware Interrupt

A signal from a hardware device connected to a PC system that causes the CPU and computer program to act on an event that requires software manipulation, such as controlling mouse movements, accepting keyboard input, or transferring a data file through a serial I/O port.

Hercules

A medium resolution monochrome graphics and text display system designed by Hercules Technology offering compatibility with IBM monochrome text. Hercules-specific graphics display is supported by many programs as a low cost alternative and improvement to CGA displays, before EGA was defined.

Hexadecimal

A base-16 numbering system made up of 4 digits or bits of information, where the least significant place equals one and the most significant place equals eight. A hexadecimal or 'hex' number is represented as the numbers 0-9 and letters A-F, for the numerical range 0-15 as 0-F. A byte of hex information can represent from 0 to 255 different items, as 00 to FF.

High Memory Area or HMA

A 64kbyte region of memory above the 1 megabyte address range created by HIMEM.SYS or a similar memory utility. The HMA can be used by one program for program storage, leaving more space available in the DOS or low memory area from 0-640k.

Host adapter

A built-in or add-in card interface between a device, such as a SCSI hard disk or CD-ROM drive, and the I/O bus of a computer system. A host adapter typically does not provide control functions, instead

acting only as an address and signal conversion and routing circuit.

IBM PC-compatible

A description of a personal computer system that provides the minimum functions and features of the original IBM PC system, and is capable of running the same software and using the same hardware devices.

IDE

Integrated Drive Electronics. A standards definition for the interconnection of high-speed disk drives where the controller and drive circuits are together on the disk drive, and interconnect to the PC I/O system through a special adapter card. This standard is an alternative to earlier MFM, ESDI and SCSI drive interfaces, and is also part of the ATA-standard.

I/O or Input/Output

The capability or process of software or hardware to accept or transfer data between computer programs or devices.

Interrupt

See Hardware Interrupt, IRQ, and Software Interrupt.

IRQ

Interrupt ReQuest. This is a set of hardware signals available on the PC add-in card connections which can request prompt attention by the CPU when data must be transferred to/from add-in devices and the CPU or memory.

ISA

Industry Standard Architecture. The term given to the IBM PC, XT and AT respective 8 and 16-bit PC bus systems. Non-32-bit, non IBM MicroChannel Architecture systems are generally ISA systems.

Kilobyte (Kbyte, or KB)

A unit of measure referring to 1,024 bytes or 8,192 bits of information, storage space or memory.

LIMS (Lotus-Intel-Microsoft Standard)

See Expanded Memory.

Loading high

An expression for the function of placing a device driver or executable program in a high (XMS, above 1 megabyte) or upper memory area (between 640k and 1 megabyte.) This operation is performed by a DEVICEHIGH or LOADHIGH (DOS) statement in the CONFIG.SYS or AUTOEXEC.BAT file. High memory areas are created by special memory manager programs such as EMM386 (provided with versions of DOS) and Quarterdeck's QEMM386.

Local Bus™

A processor to I/O device interface alternative to the PC's standard I/O bus connections, providing extremely fast transfer of data and control signals between a device and the CPU. It is commonly used for video cards and disk drive interfaces to enhance system performance. Local Bus is a trademark of the Video Electronics Standards Association.

Logical Devices

A hardware device that is referred to in DOS or applications by a name or abbreviation that represents a hardware address assignment, rather than by its actual physical address. The physical address for a logical device may be different. Logical device assignments are based on rules established by IBM and the ROM BIOS at boot up.

Logical Drive

A portion of a disk drive assigned as a smaller partition of larger physical disk drive. Also a virtual or non-disk drive created and managed through special software. RAM drives (created with RAMDRIVE.SYS or VDISK.SYS) or compressed disk/file areas (such as those created by Stacker, DoubleDisk or SuperStor) are also logical drives. A 40 megabyte disk drive partitioned as drives C: and D: is said to have two logical drives. That same disk with one drive area referred to as C: has only one logical drive, coincident with the entire physical drive area. DOS may use up to 26 logical drives. Logical drives may also appear as drives on a network server, or mapped by the DOS ASSIGN or SUBST programs.

Loopback plug

A connector specifically wired to return an outgoing signal to an input signal line for the purpose of detecting if the output signal is active or not, as sensed at the input line.

Lower memory

See DOS memory.

Math coprocessor

An integrated circuit designed to accompany a computer's main CPU and speed floating point and complex math functions that would normally take a long time if done with software and the main CPU. Allows the main CPU to perform other work during these math operations.

MCGA

Multi-Color Graphics Array. An implementation of CGA built-into IBM PS/2 Model 25 and 30 systems using an IBM analog monitor and providing some enhancements for higher resolution display and gray-scale shading for monochrome monitors.

MDA

Monochrome Display Adapter. The first IBM PC video system, providing text-only on a one-color (green or amber) display. If you have one of these adapters you own an 'antique'!

Megabyte (Mbyte or MB)

A unit of measure referring to 1,024 kilobytes or 1,048,576 bytes of information, storage space or memory. One megabyte contains 8,388,608 bits of information. One megabyte is also the memory address limit of a PC or XT-class computer using an 8088, 8086, V20 or V30 CPU chip. A megabyte is 0.001 Gigabytes.

Megahertz

A measure of frequency in millions of cycles per second. The speed of a computer system's main CPU clock is rated in megahertz.

Memory

Computer information storage area made up of chips (integrated circuits) or other components, which may include disk drives. Personal computers use many types of memory, from dynamic RAM chips for temporary DOS, Extended, Expanded and video memory, to static RAM chips for CPU instruction caching, to memory cartridges and disk drives for program and data storage.

MHz

See Megahertz.

Micro Channel™

Micro Channel Architecture. IBM's system board and adapter card standards for the PS/2 (Personal System/2) series of computers. This is a non-ISA bus system requiring the use of different adapter cards and special configuration information than are used on early PC, XT and AT compatible systems.

Microprocessor

A computer central processing unit contained within one integrated circuit chip package.

MIDI

Musical Instrument Device Interface. An industry standard for hardware and software connections, control and data transfer between like-equipped musical instruments and computer systems.

Modem

An abbreviation for MOdulator DEModulator. A hardware device used to convert digital signals to analog tones, and analog tones to digital signals used primarily for the transmission of data between computers across telephone lines.

Motherboard

The main component or system board of your computer system. It contains the necessary connectors, components and interface circuits required for communications between the CPU, memory and I/O devices. Also known as the system board.

Multitasking

The process of software control over memory and CPU tasks allowing the swapping of programs and data between active memory and CPU use to a paused or non-executing mode in a reserved memory area, while another program is placed in active memory and execution mode. The switching of tasks may be assigned different time values for how much of the processor time each program gets or requires. The program you see on-screen is said to be operating in the foreground and typically gets the most CPU time while any programs you may not see are said to be operating in the background, usually getting less CPU time. DESQview and Windows are two examples of multitasking software in common use on PCs.

Network

The connection of multiple systems, together, or to a central distribution point, for the purpose of information or resource sharing.

Network Interface Card

An add-in card or external adapter unit used to connect a workstation (PC system) to a common network or distribution system.

NIC

See Network Interface Card.

Online services

These are typically commercial operations much like a BBS that charge for the time and services used while connected. Most online services use large computers designed to handle multiple users and types of operations. These services provide electronic mail, computer and software support conferences, online game playing, file libraries for uploading and downloading public-domain and shareware programs. Often familiar communities or groups of users form in the conferences making an online service a favorite or familiar places for people to gather. Access to these systems is typically by modem, to either a local data network access number, through a WATS or direct toll line. UNISON, Delphi, GEnie, America Online, Prodigy and CompuServe are among the many online services available in the U.S. and much of the world at large.

Operating system

See Disk Operating System.

OS/2™

A 32-bit operating system, multitasking control and graphical-user-interface developed by Microsoft, currently sold and supported by IBM. OS/2 allows the simultaneous operation of many DOS, Windows and OS/2-specific applications programs.

Page frame

The location in DOS/PC system memory (between 640k and 1 megabyte) where Expanded Memory is accessed.

Parallel I/O

A method of transferring data between devices or portions of a computer where 8 or more bits of information are sent in one cycle or operation. Parallel transfers require 8 or more wires to move the information. At speeds from 12,000 to 92,000 bytes per second or faster, this method is faster than the serial transfer of data where one bit of information follows another. Commonly used for the printer port on PCs.

Parallel Port

A computer's parallel I/O (LPT) connection, built-into the system board, or provided by an add-in card.

Parameter

Information provided when calling or within a program specifying how or when it is to run with which files, disks, paths, or similar attributes.

PC

The first model designation for IBM's family of personal computers. This model provided 64-256k of RAM on the System Board, a cassette tape adapter as an alternative to diskette storage, and 5 add-in card slots. The term generally refers to all IBM-PC-compatible models, and has gained popular use as a generic term referring to all forms, makes and models for personal computing.

PC-compatible

See IBM PC-compatible and AT-compatible.

PCI

See Peripheral Component Interconnect.

PCMCIA

Personal Computer Memory Card Industry Association. An I/O interconnect definition used for memory cards, disk drives, modems, network and other connections to portable computers.

Pentium™

An 64-bit Intel microprocessor capable of operating at 90-100MHz, containing a 16kByte instruction cache, floating point processor, and several internal features for extremely fast program operations.

Peripheral

A hardware device internal or external to a computer that is not necessarily required for basic computer functions. Printers, modems, document scanners, and pointing devices are peripherals to a computer.

Peripheral Component Interconnect

PCI. An Intel-developed standard interface between the CPU and I/O devices providing enhanced system performance. PCI is typically used for video and disk drive interconnections to the CPU.

Physical drive

The actual disk drive hardware unit, as a specific drive designation (A:, B:, or C:, etc.), or containing multiple logical drives, as with a single hard drive partitioned to have logical drives C:, D: and so on. Most systems or controllers provide for two to four physical floppy diskette drives, and up to two physical hard disk drives, which may have several logical drive partitions.

Port address

The physical address within the computer's memory range that a hardware device is set to decode and allow access to its services through.

POST

Power On Self Test. A series of hardware tests run on your PC when power is turned on to the system. POST surveys installed memory and equipment, storing and using this information for boot-up and subsequent use by DOS and applications programs. POST will provide either speaker beep messages or video display messages, or both, if it encounters errors in the system during testing and boot-up.

Prompt

A visual indication that a program or the computer is ready for input or commands. The native DOS prompt for input is shown as the a disk drive letter and "right arrow" or 'caret' character (C>). The DOS prompt may be changed with the DOS PROMPT internal command, to indicate the current drive and directory, include a user name, the date or time, or more creatively, flags or colored patterns.

PS/2 ™

Personal System/2. A new series of IBM personal computer systems using new designs, bus and adapter technologies. Early models did not support the many existing PC-compatible cards and display peripherals, though IBM has provided later models that maintain their earlier ISA expansion capabilities.

RAM

Random Access Memory. A storage area that information can be send to and taken from by addressing specific locations in any order at any time. The memory in your PC and even the disk drives are a form of random access memory, though the memory is most commonly referred to as the RAM. RAM memory chips come in two forms, the more common Dynamic RAM (DRAM) which must be refreshed often in order to retain the information stored in it, and Static RAM which can retain information without refreshing, saving power and time. RAM memory chips are referred to by their storage capacity and maximum speed of operation in the part numbers assigned to them. Chips with 16kByte and 64kByte capacity were common in early PCs, but 256kByte and 1 megabyte chips are most common.

RETURN (<Return>)

See ENTER key.

ROM

Read-Only Memory. This is a type of memory chip that is preprogrammed with instructions or information specific to the computer type or device it is used in. All PCs have a ROM-based BIOS that holds the initial boot-up instructions that are used when your computer is first turned on or when a warm-boot is issued. Some video and disk adapters contain a form of ROM-based program that replaces or assists the PC BIOS or DOS in using a particular adapter.

ROM BIOS

The ROM-chip based start-up or controlling program for a computer system or peripheral device. *See also* BIOS and ROM.

Root directory

The first directory area on any disk media. The DOS command processor, and any CONFIG.SYS or AUTOEXEC.BAT file must typically reside in the Root directory of a bootable disk. The Root directory has space for a fixed number of entries, which may be files or sub-directories. A hard disk Root directory may contain up to 512 files or sub-directory entries, the size of which is limited only by the capacity of the disk drive. Sub-directories may have nearly unlimited numbers of entries.

SCSI

Small Computer System Interface. An interface specification for interconnecting peripheral devices to a computer bus. SCSI allows for attaching multiple high-speed devices such as disk and tape drives through a single 50-pin cable.

Serial I/O

A method of transferring data between two devices one bit at a time, usually within a predetermined frame of bits that makes up a character, plus transfer control information (start and stop or beginning and end of character information). Modems and many printers use serial data transfer. One-way serial transfer can be done on as few as two wires, with two-way transfers requiring as few as three wires. Transfer speeds of 110 to 115,000 bits (11 to 11,500 characters) per second are possible through a PC serial port.

Serial Port

A computer's serial I/O (COM) connection, built-into the system

board, or provided by an add-in card.

Shadow RAM

A special memory configuration that remaps some or all of the information stored in BIOS and adapter ROM chips to faster dedicated RAM chips. This feature is controllable on many PC systems that have it, allowing you to use memory management software to provide this and other features.

Software Interrupt

A (nonhardware) signal or command from a currently executing program that causes the CPU and computer program to act on an event that requires special attention, such as the completion of a routine operation or the execution of a new function. Many software interrupt services are predefined and available through the system BIOS and DOS, while others may be made available by device driver software or running programs. Most disk accesses, keyboard operations, and timing services are provided to applications through software interrupt services.

Subdirectory

A directory contained within the Root directory, or in other subdirectories, used to organize programs and files by application or data type, system user or other criteria. A subdirectory may be thought of as a file folder would be in a filing cabinet or an index tab in a book.

TSR (Terminate-and-stay-resident program)

Also known as a memory-resident program. A program that remains in memory to provide services automatically, or on request through a special key sequence (also known as hot-keys). Device drivers (MOUSE, ANSI, SETVER), disk caches, RAM disks, and print spoolers are forms of automatic TSR programs. SideKick, Lightning, and assorted screen-capture programs are examples of hot-key controlled TSR programs.

UAR/T

Universal Asynchronous Receiver/Transmitter. This is a special integrated circuit or function used to convert parallel computer bus information into serial transfer information, and vice versa. A UAR/T also provides proper system-to-system online status, modem ring and data carrier detect signals as well as start/stop transfer features. The most recent version of this chip, called a 16550A, is crucial to high speed

(greater than 2400 bits per second) data transfers under multitasking environments such as DESQview.

Upper memory and Upper Memory Blocks (UMB)

Memory space between 640k and 1 megabyte that may be controlled and made available by a special device driver (EMM386.SYS, QEMM386, 386Max, etc.) for the purpose of storing and running TSR programs and leaving more DOS RAM (from 0-640k) available for other programs and data. Some of this area is occupied by BIOS, video and disk adapters.

Utilities

Software programs that perform or assist with routine functions such as file backups, disk de-fragmentation, disk file testing, file and directory sorting, etc. *See also* Diagnostics.

V20

An NEC clone of the Intel 8088 8-bit internal and external data bus microprocessor capable of addressing up to one megabyte of memory and operating at speeds up to 10MHz. NEC has optimized several of the internal microcode commands so this CPU chip can perform some operations faster than the Intel chip it can be used in place of. Its companion numerical coprocessor or math chip is the 8087. This chip can generally be used in any PC or XT system that uses an 8088 chip.

V30

An Intel 16-bit internal, 8-bit external data bus microprocessor capable of addressing up to one megabyte of memory and operating at speeds up to 10MHz. NEC has optimized several of the internal microcode commands so this CPU chip can perform some operations faster than the Intel chip it can replace. Its companion numerical coprocessor or math chip is the 8087. This chip can only be used in IBM PS/2 Models 25 and 30, and some clones.

Variable

Information provided when calling or within a program specifying how or when it is to run with which files, disks, paths, or similar attributes. A variable may be allowed for in a BATch file, using %1 through %9 designations to substitute or include values keyed-in at the command line when the BATch file is called.

VGA

Video Graphics Array. A high resolution text and graphics system

supporting color and previous IBM video standards using an analog interfaced video monitor.

Video Adapter Card

The interface card between the computer's I/O system and the video display device.

Video memory

Memory contained on the video adapter dedicated to storing information to be processed by the adapter for placement on the display screen. The amount and exact location of video memory depends on the type and features of your video adapter. This memory and the video adapter functions are located in upper memory between 640k and 832k.

Windows™

A Microsoft multitasking and graphical user interface allowing multiple programs to operate on the same PC system and share the same resources.

Windows 95™

A new Microsoft multitasking operating system and graphical user interface.

Windows/NT™

A Microsoft 32-bit multitasking operating system and graphical user interface.

XMS

Extended Memory Specification, a standard that defines access and control over upper, high and extended memory on 286 and higher computer systems. XMS support is provided by loading the HIMEM.SYS device driver or other memory management software that provides XMS features.

XT

The second model of IBM PC series provided with "eXtended Technology" allowing the addition of hard disks and eight add-in card slots. The original XT models had between 64 and 256k of RAM on board, a single floppy drive and a 10 megabyte hard disk.

INDEX

W

V

X

How to Use This Disk

Installing and Running *QAInfo*

First, create a new subdirectory for QAInfo on your disk drive (assuming it's drive C:). Key in:

    md qainfo[Enter]

Then copy the QAInfo files from the diskette (assuming it's drive A:, but it may be drive B: for you) to this new subdirectory by keying in:

    copy a:\qainfo.* c:\qainfo[Enter]

Then change to the new subdirectory:

    cd \qainfo[Enter]

Then execute the main program file:

    qainfo[Enter]

Installing and Running *What's-In-That Box*

This program and its associated files are stored on the diskette in a compressed but self-extracting file format. The program can be run in DOS or under Windows, but it must be copied to your hard disk and prepared from a DOS prompt. To begin to use this program, first create a new subdirectory on your disk drive (assuming it's drive C:). Key in:

    md whatsin[Enter]

Then copy the WBOX3.EXE file from the diskette (assuming it's drive A:, but it may be drive B: for you) to this new subdirectory by keying in:

    copy a:\wbox3.exe c:\whatsin[Enter]

Then change to the new subdirectory:

    cd \whatsin[Enter]

Then execute the main startup file:

    begin[Enter]

From here, enjoy the show and learn more about your PC.